P9-ARP-574

# Classroom
## Touchable Tables for Kids!
# Museums

**Pamela Marx**

Illustrated by Rebecca Hirsch

GoodYearBooks
*An Imprint of ScottForesman*
*A Division of HarperCollinsPublishers*

Dedication
**To Mark, Megan, and Holly**

 GoodYearBooks

**GoodYearBooks**

are available for most basic curriculum subjects plus many
enrichment areas. For more GoodYearBooks, contact your
local bookseller or educational dealer. For a complete catalog
with information about other GoodYearBooks, please write:

**GoodYearBooks**

ScottForesman

1900 East Lake Avenue

Glenview, IL 60025

Cover illustration by Paul Dolan.

Copyright © 1992 Pamela Marx.

All Rights Reserved.

Printed in the United States of America.

ISBN 0-673-36040-7

6 7 8 9 - MAC - 00 99 98 97 96

Only portions of this book intended for classroom use may be reproduced without permission
in writing from the publisher.

# Preface

Museums all over the country are rethinking the way they present their artifacts. New exhibits attempt to involve museum visitors in active learning. Gone are the days when visitors could only read and look. Today's museum guests push buttons, answer questions, and touch samples. The move toward hands-on exhibits has been especially dramatic in the development of discovery rooms for children. In these rooms, children dress in period clothing, grind corn, make fossil rubbings, and play with shells and pelts.

This trend toward interactive museum exhibits, together with the educational move toward manipulative-based learning, makes the development of hands-on, on-site exhibit programs for schools an idea whose time has come. This is especially true since the financial constraints most schools face result in fewer field trips, special performances, and educational programs. The value of creating such on-site discovery opportunities is significantly enhanced when children are primary participants in the preparation and presentation of the exhibits.

How can we bring discovery centers to schools at a time when money is tight? I hope this book provides one answer: Make them yourself. Involve students, teachers, parents, and community members in the preparation of touchable table exhibits. At first blush, you might think that you don't have the resources or materials to create exhibits. This is not true for several reasons. First, even ordinary items take on new meaning when presented in a relevant context. Second, when people begin to talk to friends and co-workers about what they need for an exhibit, an amazing array of materials appears. We all have things socked away in closets just waiting for the time they'll come in handy. Now is the time.

You can develop hands-on table exhibits on a myriad of subjects. This book provides ideas for table exhibits in nine different subject areas. Choose a subject that dovetails with your curriculum. Involve students and their families in the preparation of exhibits that your class and other members of the school community can visit and enjoy. Tap local resources that have been waiting for an opportunity to reach out. You will spark enthusiasm for learning within your students, yourself, and your community.

### Acknowledgments

My special thanks and grateful acknowledgment go to Margery Thomason, Pamela Olson, Marlene Culver, and Gail Coyle for their valuable contributions to this book. Additional thanks go to them and to Marci Lawson, Debbie Coyle, Debbie Wilson, Marie Overlock, Christine Evans, and Janet Woo for supporting the touchable tables concept by loaning table touchables, making presentations, or testing student activities.

# Contents

# Classroom Museums

*Many, if not most, school districts live under the constraints of repeated budget cuts. The educational environment suffers tremendously as a result of these cuts. Staffing shrinks. Supplies dwindle. Teachers make more and more classroom purchases out of their own pockets.*

*These budget problems threaten all the so-called luxuries of the school system: field trip opportunities, speaker engagements, and visiting cultural programs. This book offers a method for re-creating some of these "experiential" opportunities despite severe budget limitations. It is also intended as a springboard for an overall school program to develop speaking and creative thinking opportunities for students, to enhance self-esteem, to stimulate interest in science, and to promote cross-cultural understanding.*

## What Is the Purpose of This Book?

*Classroom Museums* provides teachers with a method for offering hands-on learning opportunities in school despite budget cuts. It is a complete guide and basic resource for teachers and students who wish to prepare discovery tables in their schools and classrooms.

Inspiration for the development of a program to foster preparation of hands-on exhibit tables at local schools comes from the trend in traditional museums to create special touching rooms. In these rooms, often called "discovery centers," visitors can see artifacts at close range. Some objects, such as pelts and shells, can be touched. Some, such as period clothing and uniforms, can be worn. Items such as mortars and pestles and musical instruments can be used. Others are really "viewables," to be inspected at close range.

Think of the hands-on table exhibits proposed in this book as "touchable" tables. Each one is a kind of classroom field trip. It is filled with items that excite, instruct, and inform school-age children about particular subjects. For example, a touchable table exhibit on marine life displays shells, seaweed, exoskeletons, skeletal casts, and pictures and drawings of sea life. Children can examine, touch, and discuss these materials—all at close range. Touchable tables can be set up on cafeteria, picnic, or card tables at your school.

A touchable table can be created on nearly any subject for use in a small space. The touchables are limited only by the imagination. This book provides guidelines for preparing nine different exhibits. Some of these exhibits, such as the one on marine life, can be broken down into a series of smaller exhibits on specific animal groups. Such tables can then be displayed one after the other over several months to give a longer term overview of sea life through a series of on-site "field trips."

## How Did This Exhibit Concept Come About?

The idea for the touchable tables suggested in this book began in the library of a small public school in Los Angeles where an alcove sat unused. It had been built to accommodate a computer lab, but, alas, the funding disappeared. Unused rolling trays, the vacuum cleaner, several televisions, a movie screen, and a VCR accumulated in the space. A highly visible part of the library, the alcove was nothing more than a storage closet. What message was being sent to students about the importance of books and reading when the library began to serve as a storage closet?

Members of the parent-teacher organization tried to find a way to utilize this very small, very visible space. They attempted to borrow real museum pieces from local museum loan programs only to find that these programs had been eliminated due to wear and tear on the artifacts and borrower abuse.

From *Classroom Museums: Touchable Tables for Kids*, published by GoodYear Books. Copyright © 1992 Pamela Marx.

After making a few telephone calls, the parent-teacher organization reached a very helpful museum docent named Ms. Margery Thomason at the Southwest Museum. The Southwest Museum is a renowned Native American museum located in northeast Los Angeles.

Ms. Thomason suggested that a good Native American exhibit could be developed for the alcove space using only local plants and natural materials. The exhibit would show how local Native Americans used the materials they found around them. It could highlight the way Native Americans took care of their natural surroundings. Ms. Thomason graciously volunteered to give short lectures on the exhibit to each class. The presentations were a big hit and helped to bring a bit of history to life for even the youngest students. Kindergartners were enthralled by the concept of using cattail as the first biodegradable diaper.

Touchable tables are not meant in any way to supplant curricula or museum visits. The impetus for the exhibits is to bring "mini-museums" to students at a time when funding for field trips and other hands-on programs is shrinking.

## How Can These Table Exhibits Be Used By Schools and Teachers?

*The touchable table exhibit concept can be adapted in any number of ways as a schoolwide enrichment opportunity or in individual classrooms.*

### Touchable Tables in Schoolwide Programs

One way to use this book is as the basis for a year-long, schoolwide program. Throughout the year, classes create monthly or bimonthly exhibits for viewing and discussion by everyone at school. One or more classes can sponsor each exhibit. While each class gathers touchables, responsibility for table set-up, identification, organization, and tagging of touchables, wall decoration, and speaker identification can be divided between them.

All of the tables in this book can be sponsored with ease by grade two and up. Tables described in chapters 6, 8, and 9 lend themselves better than the others to preparation by even younger students. Younger classes can work with older classes on any number of exhibits, and all grades can benefit by viewing the exhibits, undertaking suggested student activities, and completing the activity sheets included.

You can display touchable table exhibits that are part of an ongoing schoolwide program in a variety of ways depending upon available space. Exhibits can be installed in a community space such as the library, an auditorium, or an unused classroom. An exhibit set up in the library should remain in place long enough for all classes to visit according to a viewing schedule. When located in an otherwise unused area, the exhibit can remain longer and can be visited spontaneously over several weeks.

Even if the exhibit will be available for longer term viewing, it is always advisable to schedule viewing times when a speaker is available. Speakers who are "amateur" experts from the local community can often be found to make very informed and enthusiastic presentations. They range from college students to retired hobbyists to trained docents. Some of them can, and hopefully will, be parents from your own school.

Another method for developing a schoolwide exhibit program is to have classes sponsor table exhibits that are set up for a day in their classrooms. On exhibit day, the host students devote themselves to explaining the table to visiting students, making presentations they have prepared, and handing around and demonstrating touchables. Children can do this alone or in conjunction with an adult speaker.

The tables that lend themselves particularly well to this style of presentation (primarily because they can be integrated most directly into the classroom curriculum) are described in chapters 1, 2, 3, 5, 7, and 9.

You can also present tables as part of periodic schoolwide events such as theme nights or theme weeks. The table exhibits in this book are suitable for at least two themes: science night and multicultural night. To plan theme nights, classes or pairs of classes take responsibility for preparation of designated tables. All students and their parents are invited to attend such evening or afternoon events. Selected students from sponsoring classes take turns explaining their exhibits and making presentations throughout the event.

The following exhibits work well for a science theme night:

Chapter 1, *Marine Life: How Many Fish in the Sea?* explains all major classes of marine life.

Chapter 2, *It's a Jungle Out There: Nature in Your Backyard,* explores local plants and animals.

Chapter 6, *Fibers and Fabrics,* shows how technological advances and machinery change our lives. It can be coupled with spinning and/or weaving demonstrations.

From *Classroom Museums: Touchable Tables for Kids*, published by GoodYear Books. Copyright © 1992 Pamela Marx.

Introduction

Chapter 8, *Sweet Dreams: Making and Using Sugar and Chocolate,* shows how plants are processed to become food. It can be enhanced with experiments such as heating sugar (changing its physical state) and testing water density (adding sugar to water) in addition to candy-making demonstrations.

The following exhibits are useful in a multicultural event:

Chapter 3, *Long May They Wave: The History and Use of Flags,* explains the work of the United Nations and explores flags as tools of communication. It features flags from around the world.

Chapter 4, *Sunlight and Shadow: Impressionist Painters and Their Art,* explains nineteenth-century European art traditions and can be used in conjunction with international examples of folk art.

Chapter 5, *… And a Happy New Year! Winter Festivals Around the World,* explains different wintertime celebrations that occur around the world.

Chapter 7, *Native Americans in Touch with the Land,* explains native ways of life and uses of plants and animals.

Chapter 8, *Sweet Dreams: Making and Using Sugar and Chocolate,* can include a look at how people around the world use sweets.

## Touchable Tables in the Classroom

The tables in this book can also be used periodically in the classroom.

The preparation of one or more table exhibits is an exciting open-house project. Choose tables that relate directly to the classroom curriculum and present them at your open house as an outgrowth of classroom study.

Exhibit tables can also be set up as less formal classroom discovery tables. Use the table texts and touchables suggested in the chapters in a more *ad hoc* fashion than you would if you were preparing an exhibit for public viewing. Have children bring in items related to a chosen subject. The table text provides basic information for the children when they peruse the touchables in accordance with your classroom policy.

Finally, exhibits made for a schoolwide program can be used in individual classrooms after the fact. Those touchables that do not need to be returned to an owner are boxed when the exhibit ends. Teachers can then check out the boxes of touchables and use them in their classroom teaching efforts where and when appropriate.

## What Are the Benefits of Undertaking an Exhibit Program?

## Direct Benefits

*Both teachers and students benefit when the touchable tables concept is adopted as a recurring or continuing aspect of the school environment. Those involved in exhibit preparation experience immediate, tangible gains from their efforts.*

- **Participants actively connect concepts with tangible experience.**
  Teachers often relate ideas and concepts about a subject to the students' own experience by lectures, textbook readings, and classroom activities. In the past, teachers could also rely on field trips and enrichment programs to give tangibility to some of the lessons. When field trip opportunities are limited, other hands-on experiences need to be developed. The creation of an exhibit offers teacher and students the chance to take ideas, concepts, and information and relate them in a very specific way to objects in our world. This process is a creative thinking exercise that encourages participants to select, identify, and organize objects that relate to lessons learned.

- **Participants broaden their understanding beyond the text.**
  Creation of an exhibit is an active exercise that challenges the thinking skills of teachers and students alike. In the process of thinking about, looking for, and identifying touchables, a student enhances his or her vocabulary and understanding of textual concepts in ways not possible during an ordinary field trip experience.

- **Participants begin to understand the role of museums in our society and learn to appreciate material culture.**
  As students gather touchables and identify, organize, and tag them for presentation, they are engaging in the same type of work museum curators do when they create and update museum exhibits. While children begin to understand the role of museums in our society, they also begin to understand the importance of preserving and protecting examples of culture, art, and history. They internalize the idea that what is preserved in museums is not just a "bunch of old stuff." They see that museums are in the business of taking care of things that were once, and in some cases still are, parts of people's everyday lives. This experience instills an appreciation of the importance of preserving our material culture.

From *Classroom Museums: Touchable Tables for Kids,* published by GoodYear Books. Copyright © 1992 Pamela Marx.

- **Participants engage in activities that teach both basic curriculum skills and the processes of museum work.** Student participation in exhibit development teaches on two levels. The research, investigation, and organization involved in preparing an exhibit enhances the students' understanding of curriculum concepts and ideas. On another level, the students' acquisition, organization, and tagging of exhibit touchables teaches about the work that goes on every day in museums. Participation in this active process offers children an uncommon but simple way to understand and appreciate the amount of work involved in keeping a museum of any size operating.

- **Students gain self-esteem from both the creation of the exhibit and any attendant speaking opportunities.** The creation of an exhibit for other members of the school community to use and enjoy can be a great source of pride to students. If they have opportunities to make presentations related to their exhibits, the value of the experience is enhanced many times over. The process of choosing the topic to present and researching and organizing it develops creative thinking skills. The process of making the actual presentation and answering questions provides speaking experience and a chance to gain confidence. We should encourage these opportunities for children at every turn.

- **Students learn the satisfaction of providing a service to others.** When students prepare an exhibit to be used by the school population, they perform an important service. As they see others enjoying the exhibit and learning from it, their sense of pride is coupled with a sense of satisfaction that comes from providing something of value to others. In a society that needs its volunteers and values their contributions, we should instill in our young people at an early age the importance of reaching out and serving others.

  Preparation of an exhibit for the school's use is a service of which students and teachers alike can be proud. The significance of the contribution is enhanced when others, whether administrators, teachers, or other classes, express their thanks by letter or classroom visit.

## Indirect Benefits

*In addition to the direct benefits received by those involved in preparing an exhibit, the school community as a whole benefits indirectly from a touchable tables program.*

- **An exhibit program offers an opportunity to reach out and tap community resources.** Criteria for improving the quality of education in local schools often includes a community involvement component. Touchable tables are an ideal way to tap this resource. This can happen in several ways:

  1. **Local Colleges and Universities.** Colleges and universities are peopled with both students and professors. While professors may be short of time, college students have flexible schedules and often some available time. Those with study interest in marine biology, geology, biology, art and art history, and international studies can make wonderful exhibit speakers. Children respond well to them because of their youth and enthusiasm. They sometimes bring with them artifacts and resources from their campuses to display and discuss. Moreover, this type of college outreach is an excellent way for local colleges to increase their visibility in the community.

  2. **Business and Chambers of Commerce.** Companies and business and trade organizations are beginning to realize the importance of reaching out to local schools with both money and time. You might be able to tap into this resource through an appropriate exhibit, such as one on fiber or sugar. A business organization might be able to provide a speaker or offer touchables on a subject relating to its operations.

  3. **Special Interest Clubs.** Special interest clubs exist in most communities. Areas of interest covered range from wildlife to rockhunting to ethnic or cultural awareness. Membership in such clubs varies, but often includes people with flexible schedules such as retirees. Such club members should be considered both as potential speakers and as possible partners in the preparation of exhibits. They might also lend touchables.

  Some of the tables presented in this book involve plant life, animal life, and rock forms. Local wildlife clubs and plant societies are good sources of speakers about certain aspects of an exhibit. Such speakers will often appear at no cost. They are excited about their hobbies and glad to share them with others, especially children.

  You can ask local community groups and cultural clubs to set up exhibit tables at your school. Depending upon the demographic breakdown in your area, you may have a broad range of international resources at hand. In major metropolitan areas, local clubs can represent groups of people from all over the world. Coordinate participation of these clubs with the creation of your exhibit by asking members to present or loan artifacts, flags, clothing, and the like from their countries of origin. Such presentations are fascinating to children.

  4. **Individuals in the Community.** Unfortunately, the resource of "ordinary" residents in a given community is often ignored. Perhaps we think teaching can only be done by the professionals in the classroom or those with docent-type

From *Classroom Museums: Touchable Tables for Kids*, published by GoodYear Books. Copyright © 1992 Pamela Marx.

museum training. However, local members of any community who have a deep interest in and excitement about a particular subject are often uniquely qualified to share their enthusiasm with children.

- **An exhibit program increases the number of students enjoying hands-on experiences.**
  Whether a table is set up on a semipermanent basis or only for a day, its presence on-site allows more than the traditional "two classes to a field trip bus" level of participation. Two, or at most three, classes usually participate in an ordinary field trip since the bus will only hold a certain number of children. On-site experiences do not suffer from this limitation. Time is the only limiting factor and, if an exhibit can remain in its location for two or three days, nearly every class in even the largest school can have a thirty- to forty-five-minute experience at the table.

  In a small school having no more than 300 to 350 students divided into twelve or thirteen classes, one day is sufficient to allow everyone to visit the exhibit area two classes at a time. If the exhibit table remains in place over some period of time, teachers can encourage their students to stop by the table on library visits or at any other times that fit into their schedules.

- **Donated touchables can serve as a continuing educational resource for classes long after the exhibit is dismantled.**
  Many of the touchables collected for a table will be loaned items. When the exhibit terminates, these return to their owners. Other items, however, will be purchased or donated. These items will remain at the school to serve as a continuing resource for teachers.
  For example, for the exhibit in Chapter 4 about Impressionist painters and their art, you might borrow table touchables such as vases and carvings and return them to their owners when the table is dismantled. With a little persistence and luck, though, many of the art posters you use will be donated. These remain with the school. Teachers can use these posters in conjunction with their own art curricula or to enliven wall space in their rooms or school hallways.

  The marine life exhibit is another example. Some of your touchables may be loaned by teachers. Others will be collected, created, or purchased. All the non-loan touchables, which can include shells, starfish, and sand dollars together with any purchased posters, remain with the school. These can be accessed and used as needed by the teachers.

- **Exhibits serve to familiarize students with areas they will cover in the future and to reinforce earlier lessons learned.**
  Even if a subject is not part of the current curriculum, its study and discussion are valuable. Such contact familiarizes younger children with a new subject. When they reach the subject in their studies, their comfort with the area provides a sense of recognition and piques their interest to learn more. For older children who may have covered a subject before, a visit to an exhibit reinforces earlier lessons. In addition, it creates new discussion opportunities and facilitates exploration of different perspectives.

  Some of the exhibit subjects suggested here may seem collateral as they are not directly part of any curriculum. Why should children learn about sugar? They have all too much experience with it. Why should we research and discuss flags? Analysis of subjects complementary to the primary curriculum offers some of the most interesting opportunities for creative thinking. Flags are not just pieces of fabric. They are communicative tools. Sugar and chocolate are not just junk food. They are foods that have traveled the world and come to symbolize certain holidays and festivals. The materials in the body of each chapter will help you use the exhibits to develop creative thinking opportunities and incorporate the subjects into your curriculum.

## How to Use This Book

*The first section of each chapter is entitled Teacher Guidance. This section guides you through the steps of preparing an exhibit. When you use it in conjunction with the How-To Checklist in this introduction, you will have a good handle on creating the exhibit. The Teacher Guidance sections include the following subparts.*

1. **Getting Started:** This section tells you how to prepare for the exhibit project. It gives you resource ideas and identifies any special or tricky aspects involved in preparing the exhibit.

2. **Curriculum Integration:** This section gives you and other teachers in your school ideas on how to integrate the exhibit subject matter into other areas of study. It helps increase the relevance of the exhibit to students of all grade levels.

3. **Table Appearance:** This section gives you a general sense of how to put each exhibit together and how each will look. It provides some ideas for touchables. When you use it together with the illustrations in this book and your own imagination, you should feel comfortable about setting up your exhibit.

4. **Sample Touchables:** This section lists possible touchables. While some may seem rather ordinary, remember that even ordinary things can take on new significance and educational value when placed in the exhibit context.

From *Classroom Museums: Touchable Tables for Kids*, published by GoodYear Books. Copyright © 1992 Pamela Marx.

5. **Student Involvement in Table Preparation:** This section, taken in conjunction with the How-To Checklist, provides a starting point for ideas on ways to involve students in preparing the exhibit. Always involve them in selecting, organizing, and tagging touchables. Do not underestimate the value of having students (especially those in upper grades) play a major role in orally presenting the exhibits to other classes. Having students act as exhibit speakers brings another dimension to the exhibit program by providing students with a wide range of speaking, storytelling, and demonstrating opportunities.

The next section of each chapter is entitled Table Text. This sample text serves as an overview and informational resource on the subject matter of the exhibit. It can be copied for use on the exhibit table to provide basic information to visitors much the way labels in museums do. Examples of tag text for specific touchables are also provided. All of this text, of course, should be tailored to suit the grade level and abilities of your students.

The Discussion Guidelines can be used in at least two ways. They can serve as a classroom tool to start students thinking creatively about the subject matter of the exhibit. The discussion questions can also be used by teachers, parents, administrators, or expert speakers to lead discussions of the exhibit with visiting classes.

The activities suggested in the Student Activities section vary in their applicability to grade level. They provide ideas for active learning opportunities, both to students preparing the exhibit and to students who visit it. Teachers can use these activities and the two activity sheets at the end of each chapter to reinforce lessons learned at the exhibit visit.

The last section of each chapter provides ideas for finding speakers, information about the exhibit subject matter, and organizations that might be able to offer help with touchables.

## The Teacher's How-To Checklist

*Consider the preparation of an exhibit to be at least a month-long project. Here is a checklist of ideas to help you structure your efforts.*

1. Read the table text.

2. Review the touchables list. See if any of them will require particular lead time to collect. For example, do you want to call or write a candy company? Do you want to incorporate a silkworm display? Will someone need to visit a nature center?

3. Determine how you want students to participate. Review activity sheets, student activities, and student involvement sections of this book.

4. Introduce the subject to the children. You can copy table text for them to read. Discuss possible touchables with them.

5. Determine your needs for adult (parent or parent-teacher organization) help in collecting touchables. Parents can also help gather resource books, locate speakers, and so on.

6. Circulate a "Do you have?" list to classroom parents and teachers to see if anyone has touchables to loan.

7. Decide if you want students to do presentations and begin to assign subjects for research or preparation.

8. Begin collecting touchables and display containers. As touchables come in, reserve one spot in the classroom where they will be kept. Students can organize, catalog, and tag them whenever they have free classroom time. Allow at least one week for touchables to come in. Pictures will need to be trimmed and mounted on construction paper. If you plan to display them upright on the exhibit table, affix a tagboard triangle to the back of each for support. Middle- and upper-grade children should participate in all these activities.

## Tagboard triangle stand for prints, pictures, and displays

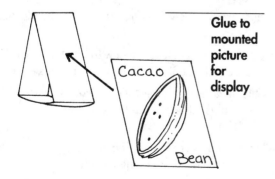

Glue to mounted picture for display

Cacao

Bean

Side View

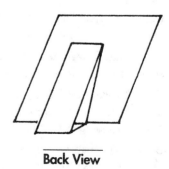

Back View

From *Classroom Museums: Touchable Tables for Kids,* published by GoodYear Books. Copyright © 1992 Pamela Marx.

9. As materials come in, children can engage in other preparatory activities. See the Student Involvement section of each chapter. Children can:

- Sponge newsprint "tablecloth."
- Prepare wall charts or displays.
- Research oral or written presentations.

10. Confirm your speaker and dates. If no speaker is available, copy table text and discussion guidelines for teacher use and distribute.

11. Purchase or ask your parent organization to purchase any posters or touchables you think would benefit the exhibit. Also, if you plan to use clear plastic sheeting (see below) to protect text and pictures on your table, make sure someone buys it.

12. Set up your table:

- Place roll paper or decorated newsprint on table.
- Copy and cut table text into pieces. (You might want to enlarge the table text on the copier so it is easy to read on the exhibit table.) Lay it out along the front of the table about where you think touchables will go. Place any pictures you plan to exhibit on the table next to the appropriate text.
- Carefully cover everything with clear plastic sheeting. (This is strongly recommended. The plastic can be used for exhibits over and over again.) This plastic is usually available by the foot at hardware stores. Use sheeting that is heavy enough to work with and light enough to read through.
- If no sheeting is used, tape text and pictures to paper.
- Place touchables near their related table text.
- Intersperse pictures or sketches mounted for upright display around the touchables in an aesthetic way.
- Check to make sure everything is identified by tag or adhesive label on containers.
- Place any posters on wall. If possible, place relevant posters near relevant table text.
- Make up class viewing schedule. A sign-up sheet may be the easiest way to do this.
- When your exhibit is over, return loaned items to their owners. Box remaining touchables along with the text sheets and pictures to be checked out and used by teachers.

## Let's Get Started

These concepts can be adapted in many ways. The hope is that this book will offer administrators, teachers, and parents some new ideas and directions for enhancing the educational environment in local schools. These new directions can be followed without substantial expense and with the goal of fostering community involvement. Perhaps most importantly, the touchable tables concept offers students new types of hands-on opportunities for creation of exhibits, presentation of exhibits, and exploration of exhibits.

From *Classroom Museums: Touchable Tables for Kids*, published by GoodYear Books. Copyright © 1992 Pamela Marx.

# Marine Life

*This exhibit provides the basis for a thorough investigation of the major classifications of ocean and seashore life. It also provides an excellent opportunity to introduce the subject of ocean ecology.*

## Teacher Guidance

### Getting Started

To decide how you want to do this exhibit, read through the table text. It provides a brief, but thorough, overview of the ocean taxonomy tree. You can cover all the information provided in the text or a portion of it. There are several possible ways to prepare an exhibit table with the guidance of this chapter.

- Introduce all basic forms of ocean and shore life (use entire table text as written).
- Introduce tidepool animals (use invertebrate section of table text).
- Introduce ocean ecology (vertebrate section of table text and seashore visit guidelines).

Survey students to find out if they have any ocean relics they would like to contribute to an exhibit. Beware that, if the exhibit is to be left unsupervised in an unlocked area, some materials might be broken or lost.

### Curriculum Integration

Integrate this exhibit subject into your curriculum in the following ways.

1. **Ecology:** Review of marine life provides a perfect opportunity to emphasize sound environmental practices and to talk about how wasteful and careless habits hurt our ocean neighbors.

2. **Earth and Physical Sciences:** This exhibit focuses on the life sciences but can dovetail with earth and physical science studies on the nature of tides, the characteristics of water, and/or the water cycle.

3. **World Geography:** Three-quarters of the earth is covered with water. This exhibit can be a jumping-off point for discussion of the different oceans and continents.

4. **World Cultures:** The size of a country, its access to the ocean, and the types of sea animals that live near its shores affect how people in different parts of the world eat, live, and use the ocean's resources. For example, Japan is an island nation surrounded by ocean. Ocean animals are a major source of food. Cattle and other animals requiring large grazing areas are not major food sources.

5. **World History:** Human practices throughout history have had their effect on the ocean and its life-forms. The nineteenth-century whaling industry, for instance, brought these animals to the verge of extinction. What lessons can we learn from these and other events of history?

From *Classroom Museums: Touchable Tables for Kids,* published by GoodYear Books. Copyright © 1992 Pamela Marx.

# Table Appearance

*The marine life exhibit easily takes two (and can fill three) picnic tables when arranged to cover all the subject matter included in the table text. Lay out the table like this:*

1.  Copy table text, cut it apart, and lay it on the viewing side of the table. This makes the text easy to read for people as they peruse the exhibit.

2.  The first section of the table covers plant life. It includes pressed seaweed displays and dried holdfasts. Try to obtain pieces of seaweed that contain air bladders. If you have no actual specimens, mount pictures or photographs you find in magazines showing different colors, textures, and sizes. Mount some of these on construction paper and stand them up using tagboard triangles to give the exhibit visual interest.

3.  The invertebrate section of the table comes next. Place portions of the table text next to the touchables that they discuss. For example, set corals and sea fans near the table text that talks about them. Arrange touchables on the table in the order of their complexity. Try to display several kinds of coral. Provide examples of both univalve and bivalve shells, starfish, sea urchin tests or spines and sand dollars, crab carapaces, and live hermit crabs. Use photos from old nature magazines to enhance the display.

4.  The vertebrate section follows. It includes pictures of fish, plaster casts of fish skeletons, shark jaws, fine-grade sandpaper (simulating shark skin), fish egg bait (or cheap caviar), seahorses, and bird feathers.

5.  The last section of the table addresses environmental issues. Show examples of the types of litter that are especially dangerous in the ocean, including cans, six-pack tops, balloons, and mylar.

From *Classroom Museums: Touchable Tables for Kids*, published by GoodYear Books. Copyright © 1992 Pamela Marx.

# Sample Touchables

Let the following list guide your search for table touchables: seaweeds with air bladders (dried and pressed onto poster board), sponges, mushroom and brain corals, sea fans, bivalve shells (clam, mussel, oyster), univalve shells (conch, murex, snail), land snails (for comparison to thickness of ocean shells), starfish, sea urchin tests, sand dollars, live land hermit crabs, crab carapaces, barnacles (found atop many shells), plaster casts of fish skeletons or plaster "dipped" or "painted" fish skeletons, shark jaws, pufferfish, seahorses, fish eggs (bait), fine-grade black sandpaper (simulating shark skin), sea bird feathers, six-pack tops.

At least two weeks before the exhibit, fill a juice bottle with salt water and a piece of mylar balloon. Students will be able to see how the balloon begins to look like a jellyfish, a favorite food of sea turtles.

Always feel free to use your imagination when collecting your touchables. Actual museum exhibits can give you good ideas; the sandpaper/shark skin comparison has been used in several museum exhibits. The widespread availability of bait suggests its use to illustrate fish eggs.

# Student Involvement in Table Preparation

Consider the following ideas for involving students directly in the preparation of this exhibit.

1.  Many children have some sea-life relics at home, whether collected on beach outings or from seafood meals. These can include shells, starfish, coral, or a crab carapace. Students can research their relics to identify them. Have them write a sentence or two about each on three-by-five-inch cards or construction paper tags to be placed next to their relics on the exhibit table.

2.  Students can cast a fish skeleton in plaster. Begin with the skeletal remains of a whole-fish dinner. Strip the fish of as much meat as possible. Pour a thick layer of plaster into a long Styrofoam meat tray, then press the skeleton onto it and remove it. The plaster sets up quickly, so prepare accordingly. You will have a skeleton cast of the fish. To preserve the skeleton itself, paint it with thinned plaster. Mount the painted skeleton onto posterboard with glue.

3.  If children live near an ocean, they can collect and mount seaweed samples. This is a simple process. Wet seaweed is naturally sticky. Place it flat upon posterboard, cover it with waxed paper, and weigh it down with books. In several days, the seaweed will have dried to the posterboard. Label and hang it.

4.  Students can sponge simple ocean designs onto newsprint to serve as the table covering. Sponge designs in one color only. Too many colors detract from your exhibit touchables.

5.  Have children find out what whale would fit into your exhibit area. When they have decided on a whale that is about as long as your space, have them sketch the outline of the whale on paper. With these images in mind, outline a life-sized whale with marker on large sheets of newsprint or newspaper taped together. Next, cut the whale out and place it on the floor in front of the exhibit table. Using masking tape, make an outline of the whale on the floor. When children visit the exhibit, they sit inside the whale. This gives them a real sense of the size of these ocean mammals.

From *Classroom Museums: Touchable Tables for Kids*, published by GoodYear Books. Copyright © 1992 Pamela Marx.

**Table Text**

*The following text is an abbreviated, but thorough, description of the classes of life in and near the ocean. The text focuses on animals that can be represented on a table by touchables like their skeletons, jaws, or shells, or by simulations such as fine-grade sandpaper for shark skin.*

From *Classroom Museums: Touchable Tables for Kids*, published by GoodYear Books. Copyright © 1992 Pamela Marx.

## Marine Life

### How Many Fish in the Sea?

*Plant and animal life in and near the ocean parallels the life-forms seen on land. The ocean and seashore support plants, birds, fish, and mammals as well as many more simple animals.*

*Let's meet some of the creatures that live in and near the sea. We will begin by looking at plant life. Then we will explore simple invertebrates—animals with no backbones. Finally, we will examine more complicated vertebrates—animals with backbones.*

### Plant Life

Plants must absorb minerals and water to survive and grow. Since ocean plants such as seaweed and kelp live in a liquid environment, they absorb these nutrients differently from their relatives on land. They have no root systems to pick up nutrients and deliver them to stem and leaf. Instead, they absorb nutrients through each of their parts.

Ocean plants live near the ocean's surface in an area called the *photic zone*. Below this zone, there is not enough light to support plant life.

Although ocean plants have no roots, they do have small anchoring systems called *holdfasts*. Holdfasts secure the plants in place as they float upward in the ebb and flow of the ocean's movement. Like tiny balloons, air bladders in the leafy parts of large ocean plants help keep their branches erect in the ocean tides.

Ocean plants are more porous and spongy than their land-based relatives. Most of them are olive-brown, brown-black, purplish-brown, or red. Only sea plants that live right under the ocean's surface are green. While seaweeds contain chlorophyll, which provides green pigment, brown and red pigments obscure the green color in most sea plants.

Kelp is an ocean plant that has many uses to humans. The Pacific coast kelps are among the largest seaweeds. Kelps are harvested and used in the making of ice cream, chocolate milk, makeup, and medicine. The kelps that grow off Japan's coasts are used in a number of food dishes such as relishes, cakes, vegetables, and beverages.

### Animal Life

In addition to plant life, a wide variety of animal life lives in the ocean, from microscopic protozoa and tiny plankton that float in the sea, to more complex animals, including fish and ocean mammals. Some of these animals eat plants. Some eat other animals smaller than themselves. This sequence of large animals eating small animals forms the ocean food chain.

Ocean animal life is divided into two basic groups—vertebrates and invertebrates. The vertebrates have backbones and internal skeletons. The invertebrates have no internal skeletons. Some of them have a hard or crusty outer covering to protect them. Others do not. Invertebrates are the simplest life-forms. Let's investigate them first.

## Invertebrates

*Except for fish and the few reptiles, birds, and mammals that live in or near the ocean, all ocean animals are invertebrates. If these animals have a bony structure at all, it is on the outside of their bodies and is called an exoskeleton. These animals reproduce by laying or dispersing eggs. Some invertebrates float freely and some are stationary. The stationary animals live most of their lives attached to one spot.*

## Invertebrates **Porifera (Sponges)**

With the exception of the microscopic animals that float invisibly in the ocean (such as plankton), sponges are the simplest of all ocean creatures. They live in colonies in a single location. Colony living means that many tiny animals live together. Sponges cannot move from place to place.

Sponges draw water into their bodies and then expel it. As they do so, they eat dissolved food that they pull out of the water. A large sponge may take in and eliminate forty to fifty gallons of ocean water a day. They breathe by taking oxygen from the water, absorbing it directly through their body walls. They do not have gills to process oxygen. Sponges can regrow lost or injured parts.

Sponges are protected by a covering of fibrous or spongelike material. People used these coverings for cleaning and other purposes prior to the development of artificial cellulose sponges.

## Invertebrates **Coelenterates**

*Next on the ocean animal tree we find the coelenterates. These animals include corals, jellyfish, and sea anemones. Some of these animals are stationary and some (like the jellyfish) are free floating and mobile. These animals have in common a central digestive cavity.*

### Coral

There are different kinds of coral, but most live in colonies like the sponges. The exoskeletons (external skeletons) of a group of living coral animals are what we commonly think of as coral. It is this outer covering that people buy in gift shops for decoration. The animals that live within these exoskeletons often look like very tiny sea anemones.

Coral usually lives in warm shallow waters. Some grow and grow to become great reefs and islands. These tiny animals feed on microscopic plants and animals floating by in the ocean waters.

Sea fans are a horny coral. The *polyps,* or animals that live within the fan structure, are small and have eight tentacles. These animals contract when disturbed and seem to disappear. While a sea fan looks like an ocean plant, it is really the protective covering of many different animals that live together.

### Sea Anemones

Sea anemones are sometimes called ocean flowers even though they are really animals. They have tentacles around a mouth cavity. The tentacles contract when danger is near. These tentacles sting small fish floating by in the water. The anemone eats the stunned fish. Sea anemones do not float in the water; rather, they settle in their larval state on a fixed surface and live in that place during their lives.

*From Classroom Museums: Touchable Tables for Kids,* published by GoodYear Books. Copyright © 1992 Pamela Marx.

From *Classroom Museums: Touchable Tables for Kids*, published by GoodYear Books. Copyright © 1992 Pamela Marx.

# Invertebrates Mollusks

*The mollusks are a group of sea animals, most of which grow shells. Many varieties are collected from the ocean floor for us to eat. There are basically two types of mollusks—univalves and bivalves. Univalves, such as sea snails, whelks, and conches, grow a single, spiral-shape shell. Bivalves, such as clams, oysters, and mussels, grow two shells that are mirror images of each other. They are held together by body tissue.*

*The shells that mollusks develop are thicker and stronger than those of their land-based relatives. Because there is more calcium in ocean water than in air, their shells grow thick and hard.*

*Mollusks feed by allowing water to flow through their bodies. They take plankton and other tiny animals and debris from the water. Mollusks are more complicated than sponges, and they breathe with gills. Oxygen passes from the water into blood vessels in the gills. These blood vessels distribute the oxygen to the rest of the animal's body.*

*Some mollusks make their homes in the mud or sand. Others burrow into rocks and wood.*

## Bivalves

In bivalves, the hinged part of the shell is known as the *beak*. When undisturbed, bivalves extend siphons and a foot into their surroundings. The foot helps them move from place to place. The siphons help them absorb food and oxygen and eliminate waste. Water comes in the siphons and moves through the gills.

Bivalves have more complicated bodies than sponges or coelenterates. While they have no head or tentacles, they do have gills, a liver, kidneys, a heart, and a food canal. These animals are not sufficiently developed to have a brain, but they have collections of nerve cells that help direct and control their bodily functions.

Bivalves are affected by the changes in tide. They have adopted mechanisms for surviving in the air at low tide until the water returns at high tide. Bivalves that live on pilings or rocks (such as mussels and oysters) close their shells tightly to avoid drying out in the air at low tide. Bivalves that move around freely (such as some clams) dig into the sand or mud with their feet until high tide returns.

Many people eat clams, mussels, and oysters. They must be taken for eating, however, only from unpolluted waters. This is because these animals absorb their food from the waters in which they live. If the waters are polluted, these animals absorb these poisons as well and can be unsafe to eat.

Sometimes certain natural conditions in the ocean affect the edibility of shellfish. For example, you cannot eat Pacific mussels from May to October. During this period, a microorganism in the ocean waters called *red tide* makes mussels unsafe to eat.

## Univalves

Sea snails are common univalves. Their bodies have a foot and siphon like the bivalves and a head with two tentacles. Sea snails also have a brain. They look much like land snails. A "snail's pace" for a sea snail is two inches per minute. These animals exist in both plant- and animal-eating species.

The abalone is a univalve that lives in one of the ocean's most beautiful shells. Many people prize the meat of abalone as a seafood. As a result, abalone have been so hunted that they are now subject to regulation. This protects the animal from overharvesting and potential endangerment of the species.

## Other Mollusks

Some mollusks do not have shells. Two very different types of mollusks are the octopus and the squid. These animals are called *cephalopods*. They have soft bodies and brains located in the head region. For protection and camouflage, they both spray a dark, inky substance into the water to help them escape from pursuing predators. The octopus is a shy animal, but is also a very intelligent invertebrate.

## Invertebrates **Echinoderms**

*Limy plates cover most echinoderms. Spines sometimes cover these plates. Echinoderms have and use tube feet to move and to collect food. This group includes starfish, sea urchins, sand dollars, and sea cucumbers.*

*Adult echinoderms exhibit a starlike pattern. Some of them have radiating arms. Many, such as the starfish, use tiny tube feet to move about and find food. These feet are connected to an internal system of tubes through which ocean water flows.*

### Starfish

The starfish is a meat-eating ocean animal. It feeds mostly on bivalves such as clams. The starfish wraps itself around a clam or oyster and exerts a slow pressure until the bivalve's strength gives out and its shell opens. The starfish then pushes its stomach out to eat the soft tissue in the opened shell.

The starfish moves about easily by extending and retracting its tube feet. Adult starfish have 10,000 to 40,000 tube feet.

### Sea Urchins

Spines cover the live sea urchin's round exoskeleton. These spines protect the animal and help in movement. When the urchin dies, its spines loosen and fall off. The round sea urchin skeleton is called a *test*. The soft inner tissues of the urchin secrete the protective test.

The sea urchin's mouth is surrounded by ten tentacles which are like tube feet. The mouth itself contains five white, bony teeth. Most sea urchins use these teeth to scrape algae off rocks, to drill holes in bivalve shells, and to scrape out the bivalves' soft insides for food.

## Invertebrates **Crustaceans**

Crustaceans are also well-known coastal animals. Many of the larger varieties, such as rock crabs and lobsters, are popular seafoods.

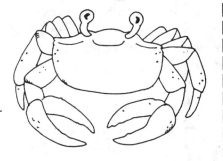

Crustaceans are members of the arthropod family. Land arthropods include insects, spiders, and millipedes. Like their land-loving relatives, ocean arthropods have bilaterally symmetrical bodies. This means that, when viewed from the head down, both sides of the animal's body are the same.

A lightweight substance called chitin protects the crustacean's soft tissues. As the animal grows, it periodically molts this covering and develops a new one. Some crustaceans breathe with gills and some are air breathers.

A crustacean's body is made up of three parts—head, thorax, and abdomen. The head holds the eyes and antennae. The thorax supports the legs and claws. The abdomen is the back part of the body. Its small appendages sometimes hold gills.

Crustaceans have complex nerve and muscle systems. This accounts for their agile and intelligent actions. In addition to the protection their agility and their chitin covering gives them, their colors provide camouflage. Barnacles that grow on the carapaces (hard coverings) of large crabs provide added camouflage.

Most crustaceans are scavengers. They feed on dead and decaying materials. They do well on populated beaches where they perform cleaning services.

From *Classroom Museums: Touchable Tables for Kids*, published by GoodYear Books. Copyright © 1992 Pamela Marx.

### Crabs

Crabs are the most common crustaceans found near the seashore. While they vary in size from small sand crabs to large edible rock crabs, most of them have flat circular bodies. They have a head and thorax protected by a hard covering called a carapace. Crabs have pairs of walking legs which each end in a claw. The front claws are often large and powerful. Hermit crabs are one type of crab without a large protective carapace. Hermit crabs find old, empty univalve shells to "live in" and carry about with them. If they outgrow a shell, they discard it and find a new one. Some people keep land hermit crabs as pets. While they begin their lives in the ocean, they move to land to live. They can live on table scraps or "crab cakes," a special crab food available at pet stores.

### Shrimp

Shrimp, a common seafood, are also crustaceans. All shrimp have in common an ability to jump, swim, and crawl in a variety of ways. California shrimp grow to about three inches in length. They drift in the tide, and people who are fishing catch them in nets.

### Barnacles

Few marine organisms are as common as barnacles. Barnacles grow everywhere—on the bottoms of ships and boats, on the bodies of whales, and on top of crabs, rocks, and shells. Barnacles begin their lives as free-swimming larvae. As they grow, they develop a bivalve shell. After this young stage, barnacles fall to rest permanently on some surface. At this point, they lose their old shells and develop the cup-shaped adult shell. Two moveable plates open and close to protect the small animal living inside each cuplike shell.

From *Classroom Museums: Touchable Tables for Kids*, published by GoodYear Books. Copyright © 1992 Pamela Marx.

## Vertebrates

*Vertebrates are the other type of animals that live in the ocean waters. Bony fish, sharks, and ocean mammals such as whales and dolphins are well-known ocean vertebrates. Unlike invertebrates, all vertebrates have internal skeletons.*

## Vertebrates **Fish**

*Of course, many kinds of fish live in the ocean. All fish have several features in common. They breathe through gills. They have a number of fins, usually on each side and on the top of their bodies. They have vertical tail fins. They have skeletons and symmetrical bodies. They are coldblooded. This means that the body temperature of a fish is the same as the temperature of the water in which it lives. With few exceptions, they reproduce by laying eggs either directly into the water or into the sand.*

*Many small fish live in tidepools. Their colors are often dull to hide them from birds and other predators lurking about the tidepools. There are two basic types of fish—bony fish and fish with cartilage skeletons. Bony fish have scales and an internal air bladder which helps them stay afloat. Sharks are not bony fish.*

### Sharks

Sharks have a cartilage backbone and no air bladder to help them float. They have large, oily livers to give them some bouyancy in the water. Since oil is lighter than water, it helps sharks float, but most species must stay on the move to keep oxygen flowing through their gills.

There are actually more than three hundred species of sharks, some of which are as small as your hand. Many sharks are plant eaters. Some sharks are meat eaters. Sharks give birth to live babies call *pups* or they expel eggs cases from which each live pup hatches.

Shark skin is a strong covering made up of tiny, toothlike scales. If you rub it in one direction, it feels smooth. If you rub it the other, it feels rough like sandpaper.

Marine Life

Some sharks have an interesting camouflage called *counter-shading*. They are dark on top and light on the underside. If they are spotted from above, they blend in with the dark blue ocean. If they are spotted from underneath, they blend in with the light blue sky.

### Seahorses—Unusual Fish

The seahorse is a very different-looking fish. An interesting fact about the seahorse is that it is the male that carries the eggs to term. The female places the eggs into a cavity in the male. When the eggs are ready to hatch, the male releases live baby seahorses into the water.

## Vertebrates Ocean Mammals

Whales and their relatives—dolphins and porpoises—form a group of ocean mammals that are found in the open seas and along many shores. They range in size from the great blue whales, which can reach 100 feet long and weigh 115 tons, to small 5-foot dolphins. Large blue whales weigh as much as twenty or thirty elephants. They would dwarf even the great dinosaurs.

Whales differ from fish in many ways. Most fish hatch their young from eggs while whales give birth to live young. Fish breathe oxygen from the water with gills while whales must come to the surface to breathe oxygen from the air. Fish are covered with a layer of scales while whales have a smooth hide or one with bristles. Fish have vertical tail fins while whales have horizontal tails called *flukes*.

There are two types of whales. Baleen whales have *whalebone,* or thin bonelike bristles that hang from their upper jaws, to trap millions of small sea animals like plankton for food. Toothed whales actually have teeth. Dolphins and porpoises are toothed whales. The toothed whales are generally smaller than their toothless relatives. Dolphins have teeth in both jaws. About two dozen different dolphin species live in the oceans off North America.

Many kinds of whales are well known. *Orcas* (commonly called killer whales), which grow to twenty feet in length, are actually large dolphins. While they live in some ocean amusement parks, they can be very fierce in the open sea. They travel in schools and feed on other dolphins, porpoises, seals, and even baleen whales. Porpoises are smaller than dolphins and feed mainly on fish. They are very smart. They have been featured in television shows and movies. The sperm whale is the largest of the toothed whales and was at one time widely hunted for the oil it holds in its head. The oil was used for lamp oil. As a result of heavy hunting, its numbers dwindled. Laws in most countries limit the number that can be hunted. The fabled Moby Dick was an albino (white) sperm whale.

## Vertebrates Seashore Birds

Many birds populate our seashores. These include gulls, sandpipers, and pelicans. Most have webbed feet and are good swimmers. They fly over the waters looking for small fish or mollusks to eat.

Gulls are among the most familiar seashore birds. They are scavengers. They can always eat where humans live since they can survive on the debris people leave behind. Gulls also eat small fish and shellfish. They smash the shells of mollusks on rocks to get at the soft tissue inside.

The droppings from sea birds fertilize the ocean water and help ocean life to grow. They also provide food for those simple animals that collect their food directly from the ocean water.

From *Classroom Museums: Touchable Tables for Kids*, published by GoodYear Books. Copyright © 1992 Pamela Marx.

**Teacher Resources**

## Seashore Visit Guidelines

1. Shallow, rocky areas where the ocean waves meet the shore often offer homes to many ocean creatures. These areas, called tidepools, are fun to visit if you follow a few simple rules. If you investigate a tidepool, do so with an adult and remember to:

   • leave all living animals where you find them;

   • replace any rock or animal you pickup in the same position it was in before you touched it so that you don't harm it or any animals living nearby;

   • touch ocean animals gently to avoid alarming or hurting them;

   • wear sturdy shoes with rubber soles so that you do not slip on wet rocks;

   • be sure to check high- and low-tide times so that you do not get stranded in an unsafe place.

2. Always wear proper protective clothing and sunscreens at the beach to avoid overexposure in the sun.

3. If you play or swim at the beach, check riptide warnings so that you do not go too far out for your skill level.

4. Put all trash in containers so that waves do not carry it out to sea. Many things we discard can hurt ocean animals. Plastic six-pack tops get caught around seabirds' necks and beaks and on the muzzles of seals. When this happens, the animals cannot eat and fend properly for themselves. Mylar balloons floating in ocean water look like jellyfish to sea animals such as sea turtles. If such an animal tries to eat the mylar balloon, the balloon gets caught in its mouth or throat. We can help protect our ocean friends even if we live miles from the shore. Make sure you pick up trash and debris so that storm drains do not carry them into the ocean.

## Examples of Tag Text

*The table text can be augmented by small tags located on or near particular touchables. The following short texts are provided as samples of the labels you can use for tagging a particular tray of shells or other hands-on materials. Since such sample tag texts are not included in most of the other chapters of this book, use the following examples to get an idea of how to proceed both with this chapter and the other chapters as well.*

**Seaweed**—This display shows the many different sizes and textures of seaweed leaves and stems. Look at the small round air bladders in these seaweeds. These air bladders help ocean plants to stand upright in seawater.

**Skeleton Cast**—This is a plaster cast of the backbone and skeleton of an ocean fish.

**Coral**—Small pieces of ocean coral are often spray painted and sold for decoration in curio shops.

**Tray of Shells**—Bivalve and univalve shells come in many shapes and sizes. Can you tell which ones are bivalves and which ones are univalves?

**Mussel Shell Comparison**—The larger green-edged shells are from mussels that grow in the waters off New Zealand, near Australia. The smaller blue shells are from mussels that grow along the southern California coast.

**Starfish**—The most common starfish in the Pacific is the ochre starfish. Here you see many of these starfish in different sizes and stages of development. Which one of these starfish was beginning to grow a new leg?

**Shark Jaws**—These small shark jaws are probably from young sharks. Look at them closely. Behind the front row of teeth you can see many more teeth. Sharks lose teeth on a continuing basis as they hunt and devour prey. When they lose teeth, the teeth behind come forward and replace them.

From *Classroom Museums: Touchable Tables for Kids*, published by GoodYear Books. Copyright © 1992 Pamela Marx.

*Encourage guest speakers, teachers, and even students to use these guidelines to lead discussions and demonstrate table touchables for exhibit visitors.*

## Introduction to Ocean Water

What is the difference between ocean water and lake or river water?

> *Ocean water is salty. It is also much colder in summer. Unlike smaller bodies of water (like lakes), the ocean's temperature in any given area of the world is very stable. It does not fluctuate more than two or three degrees as a result of seasonal change.*

## Plant Life

1. Do you think ocean and land plants are the same?
   *No.*
2. What might the differences be?
   > *Land plants have roots and absorb nutrients through them.*
   > *Ocean plants have holdfasts and absorb nutrients through leaf and stem.*
   > *Ocean plants have spongier leaves.*
   > *Most land plants have green leaves. Most ocean plants are brown or red-brown.*
3. How do ocean plants stand up in water?
   *They have air bladders.*
4. Do ocean plants have roots?
   *No. They have holdfasts.*
5. How do ocean plants absorb food?
   *Through stem and leaf*
6. Do ocean plants live everywhere in the ocean? Do they need light?
   > *Like land plants, they need light to grow.*
   > *They live right beneath the ocean's surface.*
7. How do we use ocean plants like kelp?
   > *In ice cream*
   > *To wrap foods like sushi*
   > *In chocolate milk*
   > *In make-up*
   > *In medicine*

## Animal Life

1. What are the two basic types of animals that live in the ocean?

   *Vertebrates*
   *Invertebrates*
2. What is the difference between an invertebrate and a vertebrate?
   *Vertebrates have internal skeletons.*
   *Invertebrates have no internal skeletons.*
3. How would you move around if you had no bones? What wouldn't you be able to do that you can do now?

4. How would you protect your organs like your heart and lungs?
5. What kind of animal can grow bigger—a vertebrate or an invertebrate?
   *Vertebrate*
6. How does the ocean food chain work? Who eats whom?
   *Big animals eat smaller animals.*
7. How do sea animals protect themselves?
   > *Body coverings, such as barnacles, and coloring can act as camouflage.*
   > *Some are countershaded.*
   > *Some expel inky substances.*
   > *Some have special structures such as barbs or stingers.*
   > *Consider pufferfish who expand on attack.*

Look at the touchables in the exhibit and use the following points to begin your discussions of each.

## Invertebrates

### Sponges

What you see is the protective covering.
They live in colonies.
They are tiny, simple animals.
They absorb oxygen and food through body walls.
They have been used by humans.

### Coral

What you see is the protective covering.
They live in colonies.
The animal looks like a tiny sea anemone.
They live in warm, shallow waters.
They absorb food and oxygen from the water.
Sea fans look like plants but are a kind of coral.

### Mollusks

Compare seashells with shells of land snails.
There are two types of mollusks—bivalves and univalves.
They have gills for breathing.
They use siphons to bring in food and expel waste.
They live in mud or sand, on rocks or wood.
We eat many kinds of mollusks.
Abalones have been hunted to the point of endangerment.
The octopus and the squid (cephalopods) are unusual mollusks.

*From Classroom Museums: Touchable Tables for Kids, published by GoodYear Books. Copyright © 1992 Pamela Marx.*

## Echinoderms

### General
They are usually covered with limy plates.
They have tube feet.
They have a central digestive cavity.

### Starfish
What you see is the exoskeleton.
These meateaters feed mostly on bivalves.
They move with tube feet.
They can regenerate injured parts.

### Urchins
The protective covering is called a *test*.
The mouth has five bony teeth for eating.
They eat bivalves.

### Sand Dollar
What you see is the protective covering.
Their starlike pattern is typical of echinoderms.

### Crustaceans
Their land cousins are insects and spiders.
Many are used for food—crabs, lobsters, shrimp.
They have three-part bodies—head, thorax, abdomen.
Many are scavengers.
Some breathe with gills; some are air breathers.
They have complex nerve and muscle systems.

### Crabs
Head and thorax are protected by carapace.
They have powerful front claws.

### Barnacles
They are very common.
They grow on rocks, whales, boats, and crabs.
They start out floating free, then settle.
They are filter feeders.

## Vertebrates

### Fish
There are two kinds—bony and cartilaginous (sharks).
They breathe with gills.
They have scales.
They have vertical tail fins.
Bony fish reproduce by laying eggs; sharks birth pups.
Sharks get new teeth throughout their lives.
Male seahorses carry eggs to term.

### Ocean Mammals
There are sea (whales, etc.) and shore (seals) mammals.
They have smooth skins, often with bristles or fur.
They are air breathers.
There are two kinds of whales—toothed and baleen.
Many are endangered.
They communicate through clicks and whistles.

### Seashore Birds
They eat fish and mollusks found in tidepools.
Their droppings are food for simple invertebrates.
Some are threatened because of pesticides and habitat losses.
They drink salt water by purifying it and releasing the salt through holes at the top of their beaks.

## Environmental Issues

How do we affect the ocean? Give examples.
Mylar balloons floating in the ocean look like jellyfish and can be mistaken for food.
Plastic six-pack tops get caught in beaks and muzzles.
Oil spills hurt and kill animals.
Pesticides make bird eggshells so thin they don't hatch.
Sewage causes tumors and deformities in fish.
Power plants warm ocean waters and kill fish.

From *Classroom Museums: Touchable Tables for Kids,* published by GoodYear Books. Copyright © 1992 Pamela Marx.

Marine Life

## Student Activities

1. Blue whales can reach up to 100 feet in length. Have every child in your class hold hands and stretch to form a long line. If you have a class of about thirty, this line will be about the length of a blue whale. This exercise gives children an opportunity to understand the size of the largest creature now living on the earth.

2. Give each student one half of a three-inch Styrofoam ball and twenty to thirty toothpicks dyed in purple food coloring. Ask students to cover these half-balls by gluing small pieces of purple tissue paper onto them or by painting them with purple paint. Then, students should insert the toothpicks about one-half inch into the domed side of the balls to make their own sea urchins. The half ball is the sea urchin test. The toothpicks are the sea urchin spines. What happens to the spines when the sea urchin dies? (They fall off.)

3. The following ideas are geared to kindergarten through second grade:

   • Students can pantomime starfish behavior with their bodies. Guide them through this exercise with the following monologue:
   *Today we are going to pretend to be starfish trying to open and eat a clam. Where are your five legs? Your head, arms, and legs are the starfish legs. Now let's wrap our legs around a closed clam just like a starfish looking for a meal. We pull hard to open up the clam. Pull! We pull hard again. This is hard work. The starfish keeps pulling until finally the clam gets too tired to stay closed any longer. Out pops the starfish tummy and slurp down goes the clam, leaving its empty shells behind.*

   • Using only your hands, show students how a fish swims and how a whale swims. Put both hands flat together as in a praying position. Move your hands forward wiggling back and forth. This is how the fish swims. Lay your hands flat (as you would on a table) with fingers together. Wrap your thumbs around one another and pop your whale "fluke" up and down. This looks like the whale's tail in the water.

   • Make up your own tune and sing and pantomime this octopus song with students:

   I am a little octopus
   Eight long legs have I
   I pull them up
   And push them out
   As I go swimming by.

   Use your arms and legs to pantomime as you sing. Sitting on the ground, bend forward at the waist and hold arms out over your feet. Pull arms and legs back toward your chest and then straight out front as you sing the words about the swimming octopus.

## Resources

For speakers and printed materials that might complement your exhibit, check with your local college biology departments, aquariums, and local offices of ocean animal protection organizations. Through animal protection organizations, you might be able to locate a speaker with special knowledge about fish and ocean life. College students and trained docents also make excellent speakers for this table.

If you cannot locate local organizations to help you find speakers or information, some of the following organizations may be able to help or put you in touch with local marine life specialists:

American Association of Zoological Parks and Aquariums
    Oglebay Park
    Wheeling, WV 26003

American Cetacean Society
    Box 2639
    San Pedro, CA 90731

Animal Welfare Institute
    P.O. Box 3650
    Washington, DC 20007

Center for Environmental Education
    1725 DeSales Street, Suite 500
    Washington, DC 20036

Cousteau Society
    930 W. 21st Street
    Norfolk, VA 23517

Greenpeace
    Building E Fort Mason
    San Francisco, CA 94123

Hubbs/Sea World Research Institute
    1700 South Shores Road
    San Diego, CA 92109

National Wildlife Federation
    1325 Massachusetts Avenue
    Washington, DC 20005

From *Classroom Museums: Touchable Tables for Kids*, published by GoodYear Books. Copyright © 1992 Pamela Marx.

Name_____ Date _____

**Which ocean animals are invertebrates?** A vertebrate is an animal with a backbone and skeleton on the inside of its body. An invertebrate has a protective covering on the outside of its body, if it has a protective covering at all. **Circle the invertebrates.**

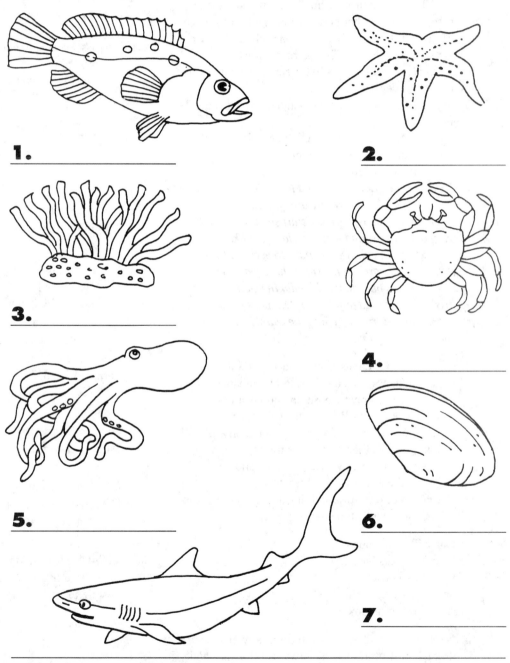

**1.** _____

**2.** _____

**3.** _____

**4.** _____

**5.** _____

**6.** _____

**7.** _____

**Name the ocean animal.**
Fish • Shark • Anemone • Clam • Crab • Octopus • Starfish

From *Classroom Museums: Touchable Tables for Kids*, published by GoodYear Books. Copyright © 1992 Pamela Marx.

Mollusks

Name_____ Date _____

**Some mollusks live in univalve shells. Some mollusks live in bivalve shells.** Bivalves have two shells. Univalves have one shell. Color the shells below. Circle the univalve shells.

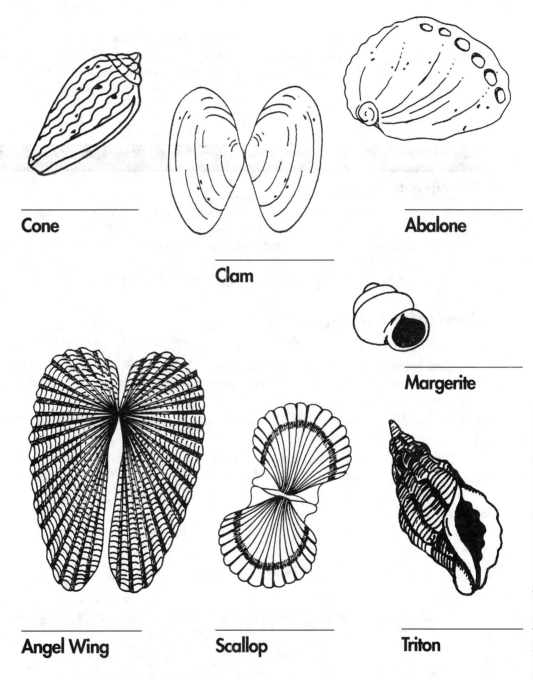

**Cone**

**Clam**

**Abalone**

**Margerite**

**Angel Wing**

**Scallop**

**Triton**

Can you name two mollusks that have no shells?

1._____ 2._____

From *Classroom Museums: Touchable Tables for Kids*, published by GoodYear Books. Copyright © 1992 Pamela Marx.

# Nature in Your Backyard

*This table exhibit is designed to open children's eyes to nature at their doorsteps. Too often, people who live in urban settings think that nature is something you have to visit at a national forest or nature center. The more we all realize that the natural world surrounds us all the time, the more likely we are to take care of it and develop environmentally sound practices.*

## Teacher Guidance

### Getting Started

To familiarize yourself with the subject matter and to decide what parts of the suggested exhibit you want to do, begin by reading the table text. The table text offers a quick reference guide to the nature categories you might include in your exhibit. Another excellent source of background information—as well as touchable ideas—is the Eyewitness Book series (published by Alfred A. Knopf), which includes books on birds, plants, seeds, and insects. Since these books rely on photographs to relay information, perusing them will give you good ideas for hands-on materials to include on your table.

### Curriculum Integration

The subject matter of this exhibit offers opportunities for discussion and study in the following areas.

1. **Earth Sciences:** While most of this exhibit deals with the life sciences, one section focuses on rocks. It offers an excellent opportunity to explore different types of rocks, the structure of the earth from core to crust, erosion, and the creation of fossils.

2. **Ecology:** Any discussion of flora and fauna presents opportunities to talk about habitat protection, litter, endangered species, and conservation.

3. **History:** Discussion of local plants and animals opens the door to collateral studies of local Native American ways of life, plant uses, and food sources. You can also integrate your review of the local natural environment with discussions of pioneer life.

From *Classroom Museums: Touchable Tables for Kids*, published by GoodYear Books. Copyright © 1992 Pamela Marx.

# Table Appearance

*Organize the touchables in this exhibit according to the table text.*

It's A Jungle Out There: Nature In Your Backyard

1. Cover any wall near the exhibit with wildlife or nature posters. Butterfly life cycles, birds' nests, and animal habitats are all good subjects for wall posters.

2. Copy table text, mount it on colored construction paper, and lay it at the front part of the display table. Touchables should be set next to relevant table text.

3. Arrange touchable items around the table in an aesthetically appealing manner in the order suggested here. The following descriptive material includes some touchables to consider in conjunction with those listed in the Sample Touchables section of this chapter.

- **Rocks:** Find rocks of different textures and colors. If you have small samples, display them in a bowl or disposable microwave dish. Larger rocks can be displayed directly on the table. If you know what kinds of rocks you have, make tags or mark them with adhesive labels.

- **Plants:** Place several examples of seeds characterized by different protective coverings and distribution methods in a bowl. Place a tag nearby that asks, "How are these seeds distributed?" Have fresh examples of furry, waxy, and evergreen leaves available. These can be displayed in empty soda or water bottles with identifying labels affixed to them.

- **Insects:** Place spider egg casings, wasp nests, and bee combs in containers with identifying tags. If you have collected any spiders or other creatures, place them near relevant texts or label them.

- **Amphibians and Reptiles:** Display pet snakes and lizards here. Molted reptile skins can also be exhibited. Try to find some pictures of local or interesting reptiles to mount on construction paper and add to the table.

From *Classroom Museums: Touchable Tables for Kids*, published by GoodYear Books. Copyright © 1992 Pamela Marx.

- **Mammals:** Place pelts, skeletal parts, and track molds around relevant text. Make sure you mark items for informative viewing. Include examples of foods eaten by local animals—a squirrel-gnawed pinecone, grubs sealed in alcohol in a baby food jar, and tubers and seeds eaten by local animals. Pictures of mammals are very useful here.
- **Birds:** Place nests around the text on this part of the table along with feathers from local birds. Try to mark and identify your findings. Display pictures of birds. Locate comparative pictures of seed eaters and birds of prey.

## Sample Touchables

These touchables are suggested by category.

**Rocks:** Collect rock samples of different sizes, colors, and textures from yards or vacant lots; small rock sample sets from local nature centers; soil samples; samples of bread mold, which is similar to the fungus that breaks down leaves into humus (to use near the plant section since fungus is in the plant family).

**Plants:** Use common wild plants that show diversity of leaf and seed type. Look for evergreens like cedar and pine, waxy leaves like citrus and myrtle, and furry leaves like geraniums and many common weeds. Search out evidence of fungus growing on dead tree trunks and lichen that grows on rocks.

Try to find local plants that grow wild. Some will be native. Others will not. Many of them will be plants that we think of as weeds. Many will have interesting histories and uses. If you cannot identify a plant, take it to a local nature or park center. A ranger or docent can usually help identify it and provide interesting background information.

**Insects and Other Crawling and Flying Things:** Samples of butterflies, spiders, dragonflies, moths, beetles, and bees can be tricky to collect and mount. Many teachers over the years have made their own small collections for classroom use and will loan them for an exhibit table.

Mount insects simply. If you find them dead, they break easily. Try mounting them by spreading a smooth layer of glue on the inside of a meat tray or disposable microwave dish. Place the specimen on the glue to best viewing advantage.

If you catch insects alive, place them in a container in the freezer once they are dead. This will keep them soft until you are ready to mount them. Mount soft insects with pins on plastic foam. Display spiders in baby food jars filled with alcohol. If you catch a spider, place it in a jar and pour rubbing alcohol over it. Once dead, transfer it to a baby food jar filled with alcohol and seal. This will preserve the spider with its legs open for some time.

Other touchables include deserted paper wasp nests, bee combs, ant farms, and spider egg casings. In some markets, you can purchase honey in its comb. Include it on the table. Later your class can sample the honey.

**Amphibians and Reptiles:** In this part of the exhibit, live animals make good displays. Even if the frog, lizard, snake, or turtle you exhibit is not indigenous to your area, the hands-on experience with the animal will capture the children's attention.

Other touchables include molted reptile skins. Ask a local pet shop to save the skins for you as their reptiles molt.

**Mammals:** Excellent touchables are pelts, skeletal parts, track molds, and evidence of an animal's residence in your community, such as remains of a pinecone that a squirrel ate.

In lieu of real touchables like pelts, your table might include pictures of raccoons, skunks, squirrels, and deer together with samples of the foods they might eat like seeds, roots, tubers, and grubs. Grubs can be sealed into alcohol-filled baby food jars or other easily viewable containers.

Pet rabbits make good tracks for molds in plaster. A pet like this that has a wild cousin can always be used to simulate the great out-of-doors.

**Birds:** Use feathers, pictures, and nests of several types (twiggy, dense, mud) here. Try to find nests made of material from an old mattress or pillow. These nests show how animals adapt to resources available in their urban settings.

From *Classroom Museums: Touchable Tables for Kids*, published by GoodYear Books. Copyright © 1992 Pamela Marx.

# Student Involvement in Table Preparation

Consider the following ideas for involving students directly in the preparation of this exhibit.

1. With park ranger or docent permission, classes participating in nature walk field trips can collect limited plant samples for pressing and mounting on posterboard. The ranger or docent leading the walk can help with identification, history, and uses of the sample plants. Even without a formal nature walk, students can gather many samples for this exhibit (such as rocks, plants, and insects) from yards and vacant lots. Perhaps a local youth group would be willing to help collect and identify rocks or plants as part of an outing to earn a badge, bead, or patch.

2. Many students collect these materials on their own. They can be a great source of table touchables such as nests, bugs, rocks, seeds, and other nature relics and are proud to share them in an exhibit.

3. Many of the specific references in the table text suggested in this chapter may mention plants and animals not common in your geographic region. Have students research and write short descriptions of reptiles, amphibians, birds, and plants indigenous to your area.

4. As with so many of these tables, students can help make the display aesthetically appealing by sponging nature motifs onto blank newsprint. Use this decorated newsprint under the plastic on the exhibit table. Leaf shapes and paw prints make good designs.

From *Classroom Museums: Touchable Tables for Kids*, published by GoodYear Books. Copyright © 1992 Pamela Marx.

**Table Text**

*You can make this a very large exhibit, or you can pick one or two informational areas to cover and focus a very effective table on more limited subject matter.*

*The exhibit examples in the following text include many plants and animals commonly found in southern California. However, general introductory text is provided in each subject area. Replace inappropriate area-specific information with information about wildlife in your area. Write regional information on construction paper tags to place on the exhibit table.*

**Rocks**

## It's a Jungle Out There: Nature in Your Backyard

*The natural world is all around us, but sometimes we have trouble seeing it because the cars, streets, signs, malls, and freeways get in the way. Make no mistake about it, however: Nature is everywhere.*

*Let's start on the ground and work our way up. The ground you look at could be in your yard, your school, or the park down the street.*

### Rocks

*What kinds of rocks can we find around us? The chunks of rock we find can be small reminders of the kind of bedrock that is buried beneath the soil we see.*

*There are three basic types of rocks. Each type is made a different way.*

### Sedimentary Rocks

One kind of rock is formed by grains of sand and rock that travel streams and rivers to settle at the bottom of the sea. It is called sedimentary rock. As these grains, or sediments, fall to the bottom of a body of water, they are pressed together to form soft rock. Some common sedimentary rocks are sandstone, limestone, and shale.

### Igneous Rocks

Deep inside the earth, it gets so hot that certain kinds of rocks melt. This melted rock is called magma. Magma collects in spaces inside the earth and sometimes moves to the earth's surface to erupt from volcanoes or cracks in the earth's crust. When the magma reaches the earth's surface, it cools quickly. As it cools, it hardens into igneous, or fire-formed, rock. Igneous rocks are very hard.

Sometimes magma cannot find a hole in the earth's crust from which to escape. Then it collects under the surface of the earth and cools more slowly. This cooled rock is also igneous rock.

The most common igneous rocks are granite and basalt.

### Metamorphic Rocks

Metamorphic rocks are sedimentary or igenous rocks that have been subjected to very great heat, pressure, or chemicals. The rocks are changed by these forces. Once changed, they do not look like they did before. Common metamorphic rocks are marble, slate, and quartzite.

What kinds of rocks do you find? Do you find smooth rocks? Do you find jagged rocks? What colors are the rocks you find? Are they black, brown, white, pink, gray, or green?

From *Classroom Museums: Touchable Tables for Kids*, published by GoodYear Books. Copyright © 1992 Pamela Marx.

## Plants

*What kinds of plants do you see? There are trees, flowers, shrubs, grasses, and weeds. If you look carefully, you might spot molds and fungi.*

### Leaves

When you look at leafy plants, study how their leaves differ from one another. Some are spiky like pine needles. Some are waxy and glossy. Some feel furry. Some are small and smooth. Some are thin, like grass.

The size and surface of leaves help them handle the weather conditions of the area in which they grow. Think about rain. If a big leaf were smooth and thin, what would happen when it rained hard? The leaf would break under the pounding of the rain, so large leaves are usually waxy or furry to repel the water that hits them.

The size and shape of leaves also help plants deal with conditions like drought. Some drought-resistant plants have very tiny leaves with less surface area from which water can evaporate. Some drought-resistant plants have thick leaves that store extra water.

*Countershading* helps some plants deal with heat. The dark green leaf tops open out to absorb the sunlight in the early morning. As the day goes on, the leaves fold up to reveal a light-colored underside that reflects the afternoon's hot sun.

### Seeds

Look at the seeds from which plants grow. There are many different sizes and types of seeds. Some are protected by spiny pods. Some are protected by hard shells. Other plants produce hundreds of unprotected seeds. Each of these things increases the chances that at least some of each plant's seeds will be fertilized.

How are all these different kinds of seeds distributed? Some just fall from the plant and grow nearby. Others are distributed by water. If a plant grows near a streambed, water carries some of its seeds to distant locations. Some seeds are small and surrounded by wispy material. This material makes it easy for the wind to pick up the seeds and distribute them. Sticky seeds attach themselves to animal fur. Animals carry them far away from the parent plant.

Now that we have thought of some general things about plants, let's look at plants that grow wild in our neighborhood.

*Replace the following text with information about plants in your own area. This information need not be typed in this format. It can be relayed by descriptive tags.*

From *Classroom Museums: Touchable Tables for Kids*, published by GoodYear Books. Copyright © 1992 Pamela Marx.

From *Classroom Museums: Touchable Tables for Kids*, published by GoodYear Books. Copyright © 1992 Pamela Marx.

## Local Plants

*Since the area in which we live is like a desert, the plants that grow well here need very little water. They follow nature's cycle. Look at the hills. In the late summer and early fall, they are brown. As the rains come in the fall, suddenly the hills turn green. The tiny seeds left in the earth from last year's plants start to grow. Through spring, the plants grow and the hills are green. In the summer, the hot sun and winds dry the plants and the hills turn brown again. The seeds fall to earth and wait for the next rains.*

*Some of the plants that you might see on hills or in vacant lots are:*

### Local Plants **Common Sunflower**

This plant has small, yellow, daisylike flowers. It is one of the taller plants you will see growing wild. It is often about five to six feet high. The plant and its flowers serve as food for many insects, including bees and ants.

### Local Plants **Wild Cucumber**

This plant is also called manroot because it can have a root the size of a person. The seeds are protected by a spiny pod and are very bitter. Early people broke up the seeds and threw them into the water where they fished. The fish ate them, became tired, and were easier to catch. Wood rats gather these seeds to eat.

### Local Plants **Wild Oat**

This is a very common grassy weed. The seeds can be eaten, but they are very tiny. They were probably not eaten by Native Americans because they were so small and difficult to harvest.

### Local Plants **Black Sage and White Sage**

Black sage was used by Native Americans for seasoning. White sage has a stronger scent. Early people used it to deodorize living areas.

### Local Plants **Wild Buckwheat**

This plant grows profusely on vacant hillsides and by freeways. Buckwheat is hard to harvest because its seeds are so small, but harvester ants are able to collect them. Native Americans dug up the ants' storehouses of buckwheat to meet their own food needs.

### Local Plants **California Poppy**

This is the California state flower. It grows profusely in spring and early summer popping up in vacant lots, hillsides, and even sidewalk cracks.

### Local Plants **Poison Oak**

This plant can cause a very painful rash when it touches your skin. You can identify it by its three-leaf formation. The saying "leaves of three, let it be" can help you remember to avoid it. In the fall, poison oak leaves turn from green to bright red. The plant grows to about five feet high.

### Local Plants **Dodder**

This plant is also called "witch's hair." It is a parasite and draws its nutrients out of the plant upon which it grows, rather than from the soil. As it grows, it can kill the host plant. As you drive by hillsides, you can often see it casting its bright orange web over many large, bushy plants.

### Local Plants **Scale Broom**

This plant looks like it might be used to make a broom. At first glance, its leaves are not apparent. As you look closer, you can see tiny leaves that look like scales. Their small size helps the plant survive drought because their tiny surface area greatly reduces evaporation.

## Insects and Other Crawling and Flying Things

Many of the creatures crawling on the ground or flying overhead are very important to us. Some are pests, but all are part of the garden food chain. Arachnids, or spiders, are characterized by eight legs, two body parts, and no antennae. They feed on insects they trap in their webs. Insects are characterized by six legs, a protective carapace, or body covering, and three body parts—a head, a thorax, and an abdomen. Isopods have many legs and jointed body coverings, but do not look at all like the crabs and lobsters that are their distant relatives. Some of our "critter" neighbors in Southern California are:

### Pillbug

These creatures are actually isopods. This means that they are distantly related to the crabs and lobsters that we eat. Pillbugs hide under rocks and come out mostly at night to feast on garden leaves and decaying matter. A big pillbug population can be important in the creation of humus in the soil.

### Earthworm

These segmented worms are also called night crawlers. They are important to good soil. They move through soil eating dirt and taking nutrients from it. This helps bring air into the soil and makes it soft so that roots can grow. An earthworm reproduces by laying eggs in a saclike ring it forms around its body. It works this ring forward and casts it off over its head. From this small capsule, baby earthworms hatch.

### Butterfly

Butterflies are insects. The butterfly's life cycle progresses from egg to caterpillar to chrysalis to butterfly. Its bright color comes from the tiny dusty-feeling scales that cover its wings. While adult butterflies live entirely on nectar from flowers, caterpillars eat garden leaves.

Some common butterflies are the swallowtail, the monarch, and the mourning cloak. The swallowtail visits many flowers for nectar, but likes thistle and milkweed. As a caterpillar, it produces a strong smell that discourages birds from attacking it. The monarch eats milkweed and is noted for its long migrations. Monarchs gather in large groups at the end of summer and travel south. The mourning cloak is one of the few insects that hibernates. In cold weather, it will hide in hollow trees.

From *Classroom Museums: Touchable Tables for Kids,* published by GoodYear Books. Copyright © 1992 Pamela Marx.

## Moth

How are moths different from butterflies? Moths are active at night; butterflies are active in the day. At rest, the moth extends its wings flat over its body, while the butterfly folds its wings upright above its body. Moths have thick bodies; butterflies have thin ones. Moths have thin, tapered antennae; butterflies have tiny knobs on the ends of their antennae.

## Dragonfly

Dragonflies are insects that spend part of their lives near water. They lay their eggs in water and their larvae grow there. At the larval stage of their lives, they eat mosquito larvae. As adults, they can fly over great distances. They eat insects—flies, bees, and butterflies.

## Paper Wasp

These brown and yellow flying insects build nests in the ceilings of garages and sheds. These nests are made from bits of wood the wasp chews to make paper. They have stingers and drink nectar.

## Honeybee

Not all bees make honey. True honeybees are native to Europe. Colonists brought them to North America in the seventeenth century. Honeybees are insects that live in hives. As a hive grows, some of the bees will leave with a queen and form a new hive. One queen bee lives in each hive. She lays eggs. Bees are good neighbors. They help pollinate fruits and vegetables. They make honey from the nectar they take from flowers. As they retrieve nectar from flowers, they get plant pollen on their legs, which they then carry from plant to plant.

## Bumblebee

This large hairy bee manufactures honey, but its colonies are located underground. It is native to North America.

## Cricket

This insect produces a cheerful song by rubbing its wings together. It eats green leaves. Some crickets vary the number of notes they produce depending upon the air temperature.

## Grasshopper

There are two kinds of grasshoppers—short-horned and long-horned. Katydids are long-horned grasshoppers. Grasshoppers blend into their surroundings so well that they are hard to spot until they jump.

## Beetle

Beetles are insects that come in many different varieties. Most of them remain under cover during the day and are black or brown. They scavenge food from the soil. Some eat caterpillars.

## Black Widow Spider

This creature is not an insect. Spiders, unlike insects, have eight legs, two body parts, and no antennae. The female black widow is large and black, with a red hourglass shape on her underside. These spiders are *venomous* (poisonous). They reproduce by laying eggs. They eat the flies, butterflies, and other flying insects they catch in their webs.

From *Classroom Museums: Touchable Tables for Kids*, published by GoodYear Books. Copyright © 1992 Pamela Marx.

# Amphibians

*Amphibians can live both in and out of the water, but to survive, they must have a moist living environment. Frogs, toads, and salamanders are amphibians. Most of them have a moist skin. They must stay near water to keep from drying out. At some stage during their young lives, they breathe with gills. As adults, they lose their gills. They are cold-blooded animals.*

## Salamanders

These amphibians have moist skin and four or less toes on their front feet. Most of them lay their eggs in water. They hatch and breathe with gills. As they grow, they lose their gills. They then develop lungs or begin to breathe directly through their skin. Adult salamanders are 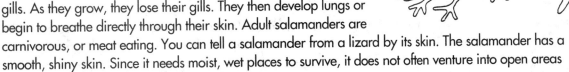 carnivorous, or meat eating. You can tell a salamander from a lizard by its skin. The salamander has a smooth, shiny skin. Since it needs moist, wet places to survive, it does not often venture into open areas as lizards do.

The California slender salamander and the garden slender salamander are both residents of southern California. They are four to five inches long, very narrow, and dark in color.

## Frogs and Toads

Frogs and toads mate in or near water. The young tadpoles live in the water breathing with gills and eating plants. As tadpoles grow, they develop lungs for life on land. As adults, they become carnivorous, surviving mostly on insects. Both frogs and toads have powerful hind legs for jumping.

# Reptiles

*Reptiles are cold-blooded animals that have scaly skins. They molt, or lose, their skins as they grow. Snakes, lizards, and turtles are reptiles. They reproduce by laying eggs. Many lizards can escape from predators by shedding their tails upon attack. The separated tail continues to move and flex for some minutes to distract the attacker. Snakes have long, narrow belly scales that help them move. There are several reptiles you might find in Southern California.*

## Southern Alligator Lizard

This lizard eats beetles, cicadas, flies, butterflies, caterpillars, mosquitoes, grasshoppers, crickets, termites, spiders, snails, and bird eggs. It even eats black widows and their eggs. It can live for five to six years. It has several interesting habits. When under attack, it plays *possum*, or dead. Instead of running and making itself an easy moving target, the alligator lizard stops moving and hopes that the predator will lose interest. It is a very aggressive hunter, sometimes attacking animals larger than itself. It prefers cool, moist living areas and is very secretive. It likes to bask in pools of water.

## Western Skinks

These lizards are much smaller than the alligator lizard. They have very short legs and live on a diet of small insects.

## Two-Striped Garter Snake

These snakes have long white stripes and live in the foothill areas. They usually live near water and feed on insects and small fish. Hawks and coyotes are among their predators.

From *Classroom Museums: Touchable Tables for Kids*, published by GoodYear Books. Copyright © 1992 Pamela Marx.

From *Classroom Museums: Touchable Tables for Kids*, published by GoodYear Books. Copyright © 1992 Pamela Marx.

## Mammals

*Mammals are warm-blooded animals. They have lungs and breathe air. They have hair, fur, or bristles covering their skin. Nearly all of them give birth to live young. Some are herbivorous, or plant eating. Some are carnivorous, or meat eating. Some are omnivorous, which means they will eat plants or other, smaller animals and insects. Humans are mammals. We have many mammal neighbors in Southern California.*

### Skunk

We see and smell these small animals. They are omnivorous, feeding on grubs, bird eggs, birds, mice, berries, seeds, and insects. They are twenty to thirty inches long. Some species have one white stripe. Others have two white stripes on their backs. They spray a foul-smelling liquid up to fifteen feet for defense. The wind can carry the smell a half mile. A skunk's territory covers about thirty to forty acres.

### Virginia Opossum

Opossums are *marsupials,* which means they carry their young in a pouch. They move slowly and nest in trees. They are omnivorous and scavenge insects and plants to eat.

### Raccoon

These animals have bandit markings on their faces. They have sharp claws and often wash their food in streams or rivers. They grow to three or three and a half feet in length. They are good swimmers and like to live alone. They are active at night. They eat fish, reptiles, insects, nuts, bird eggs, and seeds.

### Squirrel

Many squirrels do very well in parks and near homes with large trees. Because they breed so quickly, they can become a nuisance in some communities. Hawk owls, coyotes, and bobcats prey on them. Squirrels eat seeds and nuts.

### Mule Deer

These deer are smaller than species that live in northern states, standing about four feet high and weighing 100 to 200 pounds. They have large ears, a yellow-brown or dark gray coat, and a white, black-tipped tail. The males grow antlers. These deer live in oak woodlands and eat green plants, leaves, buds, and acorns.

### Valley Pocket Gopher

These gophers grow seven to eleven inches long. Their bodies are dark brown and their tails are hairless. They eat tubers, roots, and leaves and have pouches to store food. They burrow just below ground.

## Coyote

These are the only large, native members of the dog family that still abound in the wild in the Southwest. Their cousin, the wolf, is now found only in a small area of the Sierra Nevada. Coyotes have litters of seven to ten young in the spring. The babies are born helpless and are tended in a den. When they are older, the family hunts together at night. Coyotes are very adaptable, surviving on rodents, small mammals, berries, and insects.

Coyotes have a woeful cry. They signal their mates, throw their voices, and engage in yipping sessions. Their sounds are unmistakable.

## Rabbit

There are many different kinds of rabbits in the wild. They usually have stand-up ears and come out at night to eat nuts, fruits, grasses, and shrubs.

# Birds

## Birds

*The most noticeable feature that differentiates birds from other animals is their feather covering. They also have beaks and two legs. They lay eggs to hatch their young. Many eat both seeds and insects. With their curved beaks and massive talons, birds of prey rely on small animals and insects for their diet.*

*In our neighborhoods, we see many birds every day.*

## Mockingbird

These birds are blackish in color with white stripes on their wings. They can mimic other bird sounds, but also have their own beautiful songs. They often make nests of loosely woven twigs in bushes.

## Woodpeckers

There are probably more than 350 species of woodpeckers in the world. Many different types live in North America. Woodpeckers are good climbers. They also have strong, sharp bills to dig holes in tree trunks in search of grubs and insects to eat.

## House Finch

These small brown birds have reddish heads and breasts. Both the male and female have streaky coloring on their breasts. The bird is common both in wooded areas and in the city. It is similar to the common sparrow in size and shape.

## House Sparrow

You will often see these small brown birds chowing down at the local fast food place. They can be distinguished from house finches by their solid-colored breasts. A cousin, the white-crowned sparrow (which has black and white stripes on its head), migrates between north and south during different times of the year.

From *Classroom Museums: Touchable Tables for Kids*, published by GoodYear Books. Copyright © 1992 Pamela Marx.

## Hawk

Hawks are common birds of prey that come in many similar species. They are solitary birds that soar in wide circles overhead. Some species have wingspans of four to five feet. They nest in tall trees or cliff faces. Birds of prey swoop down upon small animals such as field mice and rabbits and snatch them with their strong talons.

## Hummingbird

Hummingbirds are the smallest birds in the world. They frequent many communities sipping nectar from flowers with their long bills. Their nests are small. Some species make mud nests; others use plant fiber. When in flight, hummingbirds move their wings so quickly, you cannot see them. They have a unique flying ability that allows them to fly backward and hang in mid-air while they sip nectar.

## Mourning Doves/Pigeons

Mourning doves are smaller than their more common cousins, the rock doves, or pigeons. Both species frequent the city making nests in outdoor lights, trees, or other convenient locations. Pigeons have long been comfortable with civilization. They are easy to domesticate.

## What Can We Do to Help Protect Our Neighbors in Nature?

*Many things we do every day can help or hurt our animal and plant neighbors. Let's look at some dos and don'ts.*

### Do

1. Pick up trash and always remember not to litter. Small animals like skunks can become trapped if they forage into something as seemingly harmless as a plastic yogurt container.

2. Put the lids on your outdoor trash cans so wild animals do not forage there. They can be hurt by things we put in our trash cans.

3. Recycle paper, glass, plastic, and metals. Trees are cut down to make paper. The loss of trees in forests means that small and large animals lose their homes. Landfills are filling up all over the United States. Every time a new one is created in an otherwise vacant or natural site, an animal habitat is destroyed. Remember to recycle.

### Don't

1. Try to turn a wild friend from your yard or a park into a pet. Some animals can carry fleas and other small pests that spread disease. Other smaller animals like reptiles are able to survive better in the wild than in a cage. Taking animals out of the wild can be dangerous to you and the animal. It might even threaten the species.

2. Take souvenirs like rocks, plants, or shells from national forests and nature centers. If we all take something, there will be less and less for everyone to enjoy.

3. Litter no matter where you are. If you can't find a trash can and you need to throw something away, take it to your car or carry it until you spot the next trash can. Litter is ugly and harmful to animals.

**Dos and Don'ts**

From *Classroom Museums: Touchable Tables for Kids*, published by GoodYear Books. Copyright © 1992 Pamela Marx.

## Discussion Guidelines

*Exhibit speakers, whether adult or student, can use these guidelines to help organize an exhibit presentation.*

### Rocks

What differences do you see between rocks? Are some shiny? Are some crumbly? Are some smooth? Are they different colors?

There are three basic types of rocks.

> *Igneous—volcanic rock, hard*
> *Sedimentary—layered rock, soft*
> *Metamorphic—rock changed from igneous or sedimentary by great pressure, heat, or chemicals.*

For younger children, focus primarily on the fact that rocks look and feel different from each other. They differ in sheen, hardness, smoothness, and color. If you have a smooth river rock available, use it to discuss the basics of erosion.

### Plants

What different kinds of plants can you think of?

Have you ever seen bread mold? Does it look like a plant? What about a mushroom or toadstool in the yard?

Plants look different depending upon whether they grow with or without much sunlight.

Do plants with leaves need sunlight to grow?

> *Plants use sunlight, water, and carbon dioxide to make sugar in a process called* photosynthesis. *This sugar, called* chlorophyll, *feeds the plant.*

Do all leaves look alike?

> *Furry*  *Thin blades*
> *Waxy or glossy*  *Small and smooth*
> *Evergreen needles or cedar*

Why are some leaves waxy? Why are some furry? Why are some countershaded? How does these characteristics help the plant?

> *To repel water*  *To resist hot sunlight*

How do plants make new plants?

> *Seed distribution*

In what ways do plants produce seeds? How are they different?

> *Different sizes and numbers of seeds produced facilitate distribution and planting.*
> *Different coverings (hard, spiny) offer seeds protection.*

Do all seeds look alike?

> *Some plants produce many seeds with feathery coverings that help the wind distribute them.*
> *Some plants produce a few large seeds that are distributed by gravity or water.*
> *Some plants produce seeds with sticky coverings. These may become attached to an animal who helps distribute them.*

How are seeds distributed?

> *Gravity: falling, rolling*
> *Wind or air*
> *Flowing water: streams, rivers*
> *Animals: attaching to fur and being carried, being eaten and being carried*

From *Classroom Museums: Touchable Tables for Kids,* published by GoodYear Books. Copyright © 1992 Pamela Marx.

## Insects and Other Crawling and Flying Things
## Amphibians, Reptiles, Mammals, and Birds

There are many different kinds of small creatures that we step by or step on as we go. Some of these groups are:

### Insects

Six legs
Head, thorax, and abdomen
Hard, shell-like covering
Lay eggs
Includes butterflies
Life cycle—egg, caterpillar, chrysalis, butterfly
Differences from moth
    Thin body
    Wings upright at rest
    Antennae with knobs at end

### Spiders

Two body parts
Eight legs
Carnivorous
Lay eggs
Spin webs to trap food

### Isopods (related to crustaceans)

Many legs
Lay eggs
Jointed body covering

### Amphibians

Can live on land and water, but need water
Lay eggs
Often begin life in water
Usually moist body covering—no scales
Adults often are carnivorous.
Include salamanders, frogs, and toads

### Reptiles

Cold-blooded
Lay eggs
Scaly covering
Carnivorous
Include snakes, lizards, and turtles
Snakes have long, narrow belly scales to facilitate movement.

### Mammals

Warm-blooded
Give birth to live young
Have bristles or fur
May be herbivorous, carnivorous, or omnivorous

### Birds

Feather covering
Two legs
Lay eggs
Often omnivorous
How birds of prey differ from other birds
    Carnivorous
    Large hooked beak
    Large talons for grabbing prey
    Large wingspan
    Often solitary

## Nature Dos and Don'ts

How can we help our natural neighbors?

*Don't litter.*
*Don't disturb homes or nests.*
*Leave wild animals in wild.*

How should we act when we visit a park or nature center?

*Never take souvenirs without asking the ranger.*
*Don't litter.*
*Stay on trails for safety of self and animals.*

What happens if we take souvenirs without asking the ranger?

What happens if we disturb an animal's home?

From *Classroom Museums: Touchable Tables for Kids*, published by GoodYear Books. Copyright © 1992 Pamela Marx.

1. What is dirt made of? We can find out by doing a soil analysis. Half fill a large mayonnaise jar with dirt. Fill the remainder of the jar with water and shake it twenty or thirty times. Let the materials settle. The soil should separate into layers. What do students find? Heavy, large matter settles first. Starting with the bottom of the jar, can you see the following layers?

> Pebbles or small stones
> Grains of dirt or sand
> Fine grains of dirt called *silt*
> Cloudy water with bits of wood, leaves, or roots floating in it

Let the children explore each layer. The cloudy material in the water is clay. This exercise can actually be part of your table exhibit if you wish.

Have children engage in some creative thinking about who lives in and under the soil beneath their feet. Children should think about what they see in their own yards. Some possibilities are grubs, earthworms, ants, and some kinds of bees. Some animals burrow underground, including gophers and moles.

2. Ask each child to search his or her yard, locate seeds, and bring them to class. This can be the beginning of an interesting classroom project. Classify seeds by distribution methodology, plant type (weed, tree, shrub), or protective mechanism (spines, size, shell). Sprout duplicate seeds. Each child can make a seed chart on poster board or construction paper to take home.

You can also make charts based on seeds from fruits and vegetables. These are especially interesting for younger children. Some fruits have one seed. Some have many. Some have seeds on the inside. Some have seeds on the outside. Young children have to think hard to figure out where the seeds of some fruits and vegetables are.

3. Fold an 8 ½-by-11-inch sheet of paper in quarters and cut it into pieces on the folds. Punch a hole in the top and bottom of each sheet. Ask children to think about a food chain in nature and draw one part of the chain on each sheet of paper. They can start with a plant or small animal at the bottom of the chain and work from there. Young children might need guidance. Suggest a leaf, eaten by a cricket, eaten by a lizard, eaten by a hawk. Children should draw a picture of one animal on each piece of paper. Use paper clips to attach each paper to the next in the chain. Make sure the pictures in the chain are in order—smallest plant/animal to largest.

1. Many groups in local communities are interested in protecting animal species and habitats. Some types of local groups to search out are:

Native plant societies

Plant-a-tree organizations

Special interest clubs devoted to bird-watching, rock collecting, reptiles, or any other animal group.

Some local clubs may be part of national organizations such as the Audubon Society. You can find out about many of these groups by contacting your local branch of the National Forest Service, nature center, natural history museum, or zoo. These local groups may be able to donate posters for your exhibit or provide speakers or trained docents to lead an exhibit presentation.

2. Several excellent resource books are available to help with information and classroom activities.

*Natural History of Vacant Lots* by Matthew F. Vessel and Herbert H. Wong, published by University of California Press (1987). This is California Natural History Guide No. 50.

*Science Fun with Mud and Dirt* by Rose Wyler, published by Julian Messner (1986).

*Science Fun with Peanuts and Popcorn* by Rose Wyler, published by Julian Messner (1986).

*The Practical Guide for the Amateur Naturalist* by Gerald Durrell, published by Alfred A. Knopf (1988).

*Naturewatch* by Adrienne Katz, published by Addison-Wesley Publishing Company (1986).

Many of the Eyewitness Books published by Alfred A. Knopf cover nature subjects and can give you good ideas for touchables and information for your table exhibit. Consider especially these titles: *Plant, Bird, Pond and River, Rocks and Minerals, Tree, Butterfly and Moth,* and *Reptile.*

From *Classroom Museums: Touchable Tables for Kids,* published by GoodYear Books. Copyright © 1992 Pamela Marx.

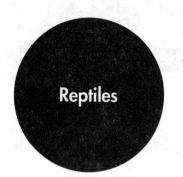

Name_____ Date _____

## Our Scaly Friends

Snakes and lizards are reptiles. They are covered with scales. A lizard has small scales over its entire body, but a snake has two types of scales. The scales on a snake's belly are long and narrow. They help it move. The scales on a snake's back are small like lizard scales.
**Color the scales below.** Which set of scales belongs to the lizard? Which set of scales belongs to the snake?

**1.**_____

**2.**_____

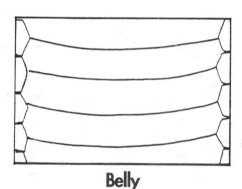

**Belly**

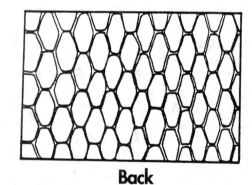

**Belly**

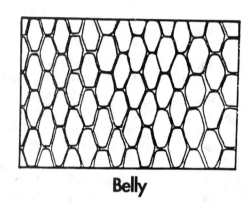

**Back**

**Back**

**Reptiles sometimes have patterns on their back scales. Can you color the back scales in a pattern? Belly scales are often lighter in color than back scales.**

Nature in Your Backyard

From *Classroom Museums: Touchable Tables for Kids*, published by GoodYear Books. Copyright © 1992 Pamela Marx.

**Mammals**

Name_____ Date _____

## Mammals All, But Who Are We?

Can you match the track with the animal that makes it? Can you match the description with the animal it describes?

**1.**

**Raccoon**

1. I swim in the water and build dams. I eat leaves. I have a broad, flat tail.

**2.**

**Field Mouse**

2. I eat bark, seeds, leaves, and berries. When young I am often spotted. These spots help me hide from predators.

**3.**

**Wolf**

3. I am a tiny mammal. I live in burrows under the ground. I eat berries and nuts.

**4.**

**Skunk**

4. I have a bandit's mask and a ringed tail. I eat fish, insects, fruits, and eggs.

**5.**

**Deer**

5. I am a member of the wild dog family. I live in a den. My cousins are the fox and the coyote.

**6.**

**Beaver**

6. I am peaceful and friendly. When frightened I protect myself by spraying a bad-smelling scent into the air. I eat seeds, berries, and insects.

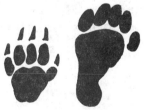

From *Classroom Museums: Touchable Tables for Kids*, published by GoodYear Books. Copyright © 1992 Pamela Marx.

# The History and Uses of Flags

*This exhibit has several different purposes. It explores flags as tools of communication and the symbols people and nations use to represent themselves. The evolution of flags reveals much about history and politics.*

## Teacher Guidance

### Getting Started

To get a general sense of the kinds of information conveyed by this exhibit, begin by reading the table text. Once you have read the text, peruse the Eyewitness Book (published by Alfred A. Knopf) entitled *Flag*. This book is an excellent resource to use when preparing an exhibit on flags. It may give you ideas for additional touchables and activities.

In one section of the exhibit a variety of flags is displayed. These can be international, state, or historical flags. Determine the direction of your exhibit before you plan how and where to make or obtain your sample flags.

### Curriculum Integration

This table lends itself well to a variety of study areas and thematic events.

1.  **World Cultures and Geography:** The table text suggests a display of international flags, but you can choose to use state flags or historical American flags. Pair the flags you use with their states or countries on a wall-mounted world or national map. Pairing flags with places identifies and reinforces locations on the map. If you use international flags on the exhibit table, you can investigate flags as national symbols in concert with the study of cultures and peoples around the world.

2.  **Language Arts:** One of the themes of this exhibit is communication. Use the exhibit to spark creative thinking about the many methods and ways people communicate. Incorporate this into your language arts curriculum.

3.  **World Peace and Brotherhood:** Pair the presentation of this exhibit with themed events or student activities about world peace or brotherhood (United Nations Day in October or Martin Luther King's birthday in January, for example). This coupling works because the exhibit focuses on issues of communication, peace, and people around the world.

4.  **History:** Integrate a table on flags into your history curriculum. Flags have been used in different ways throughout history. Furthermore, the use of flags for some purposes has been affected by technological advances. Sometimes flags change because of historical events.

From *Classroom Museums: Touchable Tables for Kids*, published by GoodYear Books. Copyright © 1992 Pamela Marx.

# Table Appearance

*What might this table look like?*

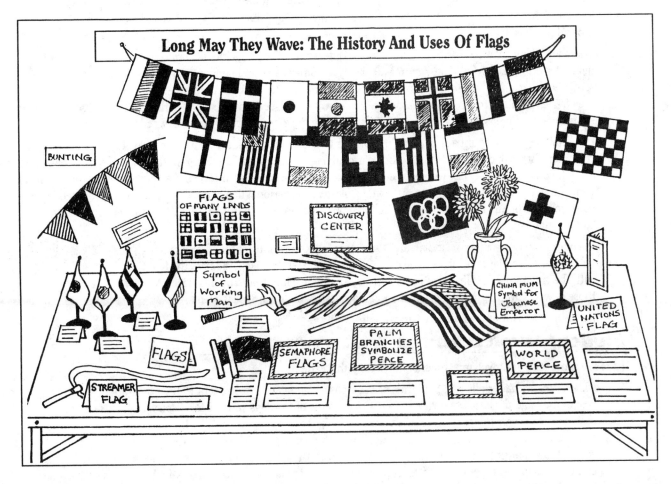

Long May They Wave: The History And Uses Of Flags

1. Decorate the wall behind your exhibit with a poster of international or state flags. Hang a world or United States map so sample flags can be paired with geographic locations. Other possible wall decorations include posters of the United Nations, posters of children or places around the world, and student-made construction paper flags as described in the Sample Touchables and Student Involvement sections of this chapter.

2. The first part of the exhibit includes two types of touchables. The first is a collection of objects we don't usually think of as flags. These include bunting, streamers, college pennants, referee flags, mock semaphore flags, and gymnast streamers. The second set of touchables is a collection of symbols often used on flags—palm branch, olive branch, China chrysanthemum, and hammer (as in hammer and sickle). These demonstrate how everyday items are stylized for use on flags.

3. Your display of various flags goes on the middle section of the table. The table text included in this chapter assumes use of flags from around the world, but do not feel restricted by this. You might instead use samples of state flags or historical American flags. Display flags with small construction paper tags that explain the state or country in which they are used, dates of use, and meanings of colors and symbols on each. The information on these tags can be researched by the students.

4. Devote the last section of the table to the United Nations. Include a UN flag. Mount and stand upright pictures of the UN building as well as pictures of children from different parts of the world.

5. Copy, cut, and mount any parts of the table text that are relevant to your display. Place them on the viewing side of the table for easy reading.

From *Classroom Museums: Touchable Tables for Kids*, published by GoodYear Books. Copyright © 1992 Pamela Marx.

## Sample Touchables

The table should include examples of the different materials and shapes of flags as well as an array of various flags from around the world, the states, or history, as you decide.

There are many colorful possibilities for display. Different types of flags include bunting, semaphore flags, plastic sports field markers, referee's foul flags, gymnastic dance streamer flags, and pennants. Display student-made bunting and semaphore flags. (See instructions in Student Involvement section.) Dance streamers for rhythmic or ribbon dancing are often available at toy stores at reasonable prices. Or, simulate them by stapling three-foot lengths of one-inch-wide satin ribbon (or crêpe paper streamers) to inexpensive bangle bracelets (or paper-covered toilet paper rolls).

Use small flags from countries around the world as well as from familiar organizations. The United Nations Gift Shop in New York City is one mail-order source for national flags. Small flags can be purchased from this shop for about $2 each. If you know in advance who your exhibit speaker will be, focus your foreign flag purchases on the countries of your speaker's expertise. You might also hang a plastic international flag banner from the ceiling. Such banners include flags from Europe and Central America. You can buy them for less than $10 from local teacher supply stores or educational mail-order houses.

In addition to international flags, create flags from well-known international organizations out of construction paper for the wall. Familiar examples include racing's black and white checkered flag, the Red Cross flag, and the Olympic flag with the traditional interlinking five circles. You might also find that students have specialty flags at home, such as those of well-known organizations and special decorative flags from local events.

For other ideas for touchables, see the preceding section on Table Appearance.

## Student Involvement in Table Preparation

Here are some ideas for involving students in creating this exhibit.

1.  Older students have skills that lend themselves well to significant involvement in the preparation of this exhibit. The cost of the table can be kept down if students make most of the flags you use for display. Students can make 8 ½-by-11-inch construction paper versions of organizational flags to hang on the wall, including racing's black and white checkered flag, the Olympic flag, and the Red Cross healing flag, which is a red cross on a white background. Students can simulate bunting by cutting out brightly colored construction paper triangles (six inches across top of triangle by eight inches long) and mounting them on the wall. Mount triangles so that the six-inch side of each triangle is at the top and so that the top corner of one triangle touches a top corner of the next triangle, and so on. Make semaphore flags by gluing rectangles of red fabric (five by seven inches) onto nine-inch dowels.

2.  Students can prepare flags on three-by-five-inch cards. These can be international, state, or historical flags, depending upon the focus you choose for your exhibit. Mount these flags on dowels with tape and display them on the exhibit table in lieu of fabric flags. Supplement these table flags with flags for wall display made by using small balls of crushed tissue paper to decorate eight-by-eleven-inch sheets of white construction paper (or posterboard) in appropriate colors and designs. Students can also gather plants and items they have seen used as symbols on flags.

From *Classroom Museums: Touchable Tables for Kids*, published by GoodYear Books. Copyright © 1992 Pamela Marx.

**Table Text**

*This table text is developed in two parts. The first side of the table explores flags in general, their various uses, their communicative functions, and their roles as national symbols. This part of the table text includes descriptions of a variety of flags. These descriptions are for example only. If you decide not to focus on international flags, print simple descriptions of the flags you do use on small construction paper tags to fold and display upright on your table. The second part of the table is a brief history and description of the United Nations.*

## Long May They Wave: The History and Uses of Flags

*We communicate with each other in many ways—by what we say, by what we write, by how we dress. As we look at the world around us, we can find messages in many things. We recognize a school by the shape and placement of its buildings. The look of other buildings tells us they are fire stations.*

*Flags are used to communicate ideas and feelings, too. Flags of all different kinds surround us all the time. Streamers of small flags announce store openings and sales. American flags fly to identify schools and government buildings. People wave flags as car races end.*

*Let's find out more about how people have communicated with flags through history and how we still communicate with them today.*

## The History of Flags

How does a flag look? It is usually a piece of fabric attached to a pole. It is used to send a message or is carried to show loyalty to a leader or country.

In ancient Egypt, Greece, and Rome, people used something similar to flags for these same purposes. They carried poles topped with carved wooden symbols or fans. Sometimes they placed them on boats. Sometimes people carried them in parades and in battle.

The use of fabric flags may have started by accident or in an emergency. Perhaps someone who was in danger or lost tore a piece of cloth, tied it to a stick, and waved it to warn of danger or to attract attention. Flags attached to the side of a pole were first used in China. People in the Middle East then began using them and introduced them to people in Europe.

The first flags were made of plain fabric. They had no design. Flags with designs did not become common until about 900 years ago during a period of religious wars called the Crusades. During the Crusades, Christians and Moslems battled. The Christians used flags with crosses to identify their armies. The Moslems used flags with inscriptions to identify theirs.

Coats of arms came to play a part in flag design in many countries through history. Coats of arms are pictures and designs that a family adopts to represent itself. In European countries, the coat of arms is usually in the shape of a shield, which is often divided into four parts. The pictures in the different parts tell something of the family's history. In Japan, these family designs are usually circular badges called *mon*. The designs contained in these badges are very stylized.

This art of creating badges and coats of arms is called *heraldry*. Families use them on fans, clothing, flags, and banners. The symbols communicate something about how the family feels about itself.

From *Classroom Museums: Touchable Tables for Kids,* published by GoodYear Books. Copyright © 1992 Pamela Marx.

From *Classroom Museums: Touchable Tables for Kids*, published by GoodYear Books. Copyright © 1992 Pamela Marx.

# The Uses of Flags

*Throughout history, flags have served many purposes. They still do today. What are some of these uses?*

## Flags for Identification

The most common use of early flags was for identification. They identified churches and homes of wealthy or important families. They identified armies in battle. Soldiers sometimes attached them to weapons. Into the early 1800s, British soldiers put triangular flags called *pennants* on their battle lances. Flags have flown for centuries on warships and boats.

## Flags for Sending Messages

Before the invention of electricity, flags were important tools for sending messages. Sailors used two small flags called *semaphore* flags to exchange messages between ships. They also used them to convey messages during land and sea battles. During the Civil War, soldiers waved one small flag in short movements to symbolize the dots and dashes of Morse Code.

Flags were also used at railway stations and crossings to give instructions to the engineer from the platform. Today many of the messages once sent by flags are sent by lights or electronics.

## Flags for Sports and Celebration

Flags have long been at sporting events and celebrations. Historically, pennants and flags decorated horses and gaming equipment during sporting events such as medieval tournaments between knights. Often, coats of arms appeared on these flags. Flags also flew at special feasts, pageants, and exhibitions.

Today, the flags we use at sporting events are much simpler in design than those of the past. A black and white checkered flag ceremoniously announces the winner of a car race and closes the race. During a race, other flags send messages to drivers. Soccer linemen throw up small flags to signal a referee that a ball has gone out of bounds or that a player has broken a rule. Flags also mark boundaries at some sporting events. Gymnasts use streamer flags as part of their exercise routines. *Bunting—* or strings of small flags—flies at sporting events as decoration. It also decorates stores on opening day and big sales events.

## Flags as National Symbols

Flags are most recognizable as symbols of countries. National flags fly to identify school buildings, government buildings, government ships, and all sorts of large public buildings and forums. They fly during times of war and peace. People carry them in parades. Children salute them each morning in school. People carry them on scientific expeditions and explorations and fly them to represent conquest or achievement.

Each country around the world has a flag, and all are different. Each nation uses different colors and different symbols to represent itself to its people and to the people of the world. In the United States, each state has its own flag as well.

The United States flag itself has changed many times since the colonists first formed the country. Today the stripes stand for the first thirteen states, and each star represents one of the now fifty states that make up the Union.

Colors/Symbols

# How Flags Use Colors and Symbols

Often, a flag carries a central symbol that relates to a belief or object important to a nation or organization. For example, the Canadian flag features the red maple leaf, a design taken from the leaf of a local tree. Japan's flag has displayed the symbol of the sun for over a thousand years. The sun is the legendary ancestor of the Japanese emperor, and Japan is sometimes called the Land of the Rising Sun.

Many everyday designs and objects stand for certain ideas and themes. These symbols are commonly used on flags.

The *olive branch,* the *palm branch,* and the *dove* symbolize peace.

The design of the *chrysanthemum* is simplified and used to represent the emperor on Japanese emperor standards.

The Asian *yin and yang* symbol now appears on the South Korean flag. It symbolizes wholeness and the coming together of opposites.

The *hammer and sickle* stands for the tools of industry and agriculture and was commonly used on flags of countries following communist philosophies. It symbolized the work of the common man. The sickle reminds us of harvesting grain by hand with sickles. The hammer reminds us of the work of building and manufacturing.

*Five interlocking circles* are used on Olympic flags to represent the peoples of the five populated continents who participate in the games.

The Greenpeace flag uses the *rainbow* to symbolize hope and harmony with the environment.

A white flag with a large red cross in the center is used by the emergency and medical relief organization called the Red Cross. The symbol of the *red cross* has come to mean healing and emergency medical care to people around the world.

Colors have special meanings, too. Some of these meanings have changed over the years.

A *red* flag flown on its own or tied to something usually means danger or beware. In the past, red on national flags meant courage, nobility, or power. Today, it more often represents the power of the people and recognizes bloodshed in war or revolution.

*Green* is a hopeful color. People use it to symbolize youth, hope, or environmental concern. They also use it on national flags to symbolize agriculture or vegetation.

*White* is the color of surrender. Waving the white flag in times of battle indicates a side's desire to give up the fight. White has also come to mean peace.

*Light blue* signifies peace to many people because it appears on the United Nations flag. In fact, the light blue background of the UN flag is now sometimes called United Nations blue.

From *Classroom Museums: Touchable Tables for Kids,* published by GoodYear Books. Copyright © 1992 Pamela Marx.

From *Classroom Museums: Touchable Tables for Kids*, published by GoodYear Books. Copyright © 1992 Pamela Marx.

## Some Flags of the World—
## What Their Symbols and Colors Mean

### Greece

The design of the Greek flag was inspired by the American Stars and Stripes. The cross in the corner stands for the religious beginnings of the nineteenth-century Greek freedom movement against the Moslem Turks.

### Denmark, Norway, and Iceland

Each of these flags includes a cross as its central design. The cross shows affinity with other Scandinavian countries. It may have Christian origins.

### Canada

This flag features the red maple leaf as its central design. This is a popular emblem in Canada, taken from the red maple tree.

### Australia

The Australian flag combines the Union Jack of England on a blue background with the constellation of the Southern Cross. The Southern Cross has for centuries been used as a navigational aid by sailors in the southern hemisphere. The separate large star stands for the British commonwealth.

### Republic of Korea

The South Korean flag incorporates the Asian symbol of yin and yang. This symbol represents wholeness, unity, and a coming together of opposite or different ideas.

### Japan

A red sun disk on a white background makes up the Japanese flag. The name Japan means "source of the sun."

### Ethiopia

Bars of green, yellow, and red on the Ethiopian flag represent African liberation. Ethiopia remained free of colonization until 1936 and was much admired for its resistance.

### Israel

This flag combines a blue Star of David on a white background with two horizontal blue stripes. The Star of David has long been a symbol of the Jewish people.

### France

The French national flag is called the *Tricolor*. It contains three bars of color—blue, white, and red—which were first used during the revolution of 1789. These three colors are used in many flags to symbolize liberty.

## Austria

The Austrian national flag is one of the oldest in the world. The red and white stripes of this flag appear to have been used since the year 1230.

## Zambia

On its broad field of green, the Zambian flag has vertical stripes of red, black, and yellow in one corner. These four colors appear in the flags of many African nations. They are sometimes called the *Pan-African* colors and are associated with liberation and freedom. A regal golden bird flies in the upper right corner of this flag.

## Italy

Green, white, and red first decorated the Italian flag during Napoleon's invasions of Italy in 1796. In 1861, Italy was united for the first time. At this time, the green, white, and red were used again.

## Portugal

This flag has two main colors with a central coat of arms. Green represents a great Portuguese leader named Prince Henry the Navigator. Red stands for revolution. A coat of arms overlays a gold sphere that represents the orbits of the planets.

**United Nations**

## What Is the United Nations?

Throughout history, wars have been fought over many things. They have been fought over land and money. They have been fought over religion and beliefs. They have been fought over the brutality of leaders.

About fifty years ago, one of these great and terrible wars raged. It was called World War II. People fought in many parts of the world. Planes screeched across the skies. Guns fired and soldiers died. Bombs fell and demolished entire cities.

People grew tired of war. And they were fearful, too. More and more terrible weapons were made with each war. Where would it stop?

Some people decided to put together an organization that would try to keep the world at peace. In 1945, people from several countries met to make a plan for how such an organization would work. These people decided to call their peace organization the United Nations. The name signifies countries united and working together.

They asked many, many countries to join. On October 24, 1945, enough countries had joined for the United Nations to begin its work.

Today, the United Nations meets in New York City in the United States. The flags of the member countries fly in front of the United Nations building. Representatives from member countries around the world meet to try to solve world problems and to settle arguments when they arise.

In addition to trying to settle arguments between countries, the United Nations does other important work, too. It encourages rich nations to help poorer nations so all people on earth can live happier, healthier lives. To further this goal, the United Nations sends teams of teachers and scientists around the world. These people teach farmers how to grow better crops. They build dams for irrigation. They build schools so that people can learn to read and write. They send doctors and much needed medicine to help those who are sick.

From *Classroom Museums: Touchable Tables for Kids*, published by GoodYear Books. Copyright © 1992 Pamela Marx.

## Teacher Resources

## Discussion Guidelines

*Use these discussion guidelines in conjunction with presentation of the exhibit table and to foster creative thinking about the different ways in which we communicate.*

How many different ways can you communicate with others?

> *Speaking      Writing*
> *Hand Motions  Head Motions*

How would you say "no" with your voice?

How would you say "no" with your head?

How can you say "no" with your hands?

How else do we communicate messages to people?

Do we communicate anything by the clothes we wear?

> *Where we are going*
> *If it's a formal or casual occasion*

If you wear the uniform of a team you are on, what do you communicate to those who see you?

> *That you are part of a team*
> *That you are going to a team function*
> *That you will be playing a game soon*
> Does anything on this table communicate a message to you?

Can we communicate with flags?

> *Let's find out!*

How do you think a flag was first used?

> *To draw attention to something*
> *To warn people away from something*
> *To claim ownership of something*

Why would a flag or flags have been used?

> *They are easy to see from a distance.*
> *They look festive.*

For what do we use flags?

> For identification
>
> > *Wealthy and royal families flew them at their castles and homes.*
> > *They also flew them at sporting events such as jousts.*
> > *They flew them at feasts and pageants.*
> > *During battle, armies used them to identify friends and foes. They were used on land and flown on ships.*
> > *They fly in front of government buildings.*
>
> Before electricity, for sending messages
>
> > *Semaphore flags were used to send messages between ships. Used in pairs, different positions symbolized different letters.*
> > *Soldiers waved small flags to represent the dots and dashes of Morse Code during the Civil War.*
> > *They were used to send messages to trains from railway platforms.*
>
> For sporting events
>
> > *Linemen use flags in soccer to signal errors.*
> > *Flags must be rounded by skiers in certain downhill events.*
> > *Small plastic flags mark the courses in long distance running events.*
> > *Checkered flags signal the end of car races.*
> > *Gymnasts use streamer flags in exercise routines.*
>
> For celebrations
>
> > *Bunting appears at store openings and sales.*
> > *Flags are carried in parades.*
> > *Flags adopted by organizations celebrate and advertise events.*
>
> For national symbols

Where do you see the American flag fly? Why?

> *On presidential cars*
> *On government buildings*
> *Carried by the U.S. Olympic team or any other national sports team*

Does it fly in front of buildings? What kind of buildings?

From *Classroom Museums: Touchable Tables for Kids*, published by GoodYear Books. Copyright © 1992 Pamela Marx.

## Student Activities

1. Students can prepare sample flags for classroom use or for the exhibit. Have each student pick a country or state, depending upon your curriculum. The students should create their flags on three-by-five cards or eight-by-eleven inch paper as described in the section of this chapter entitled Student Involvement in Table Preparation. Then, students research the colors and symbols used on their flags. Perhaps some students could learn folktales from their chosen countries. Have students work in pairs or small groups and use the results of their research to make oral presentations to other classes in conjunction with the exhibit.

2. Have students research and present the proper methods of folding and handling the American flag. Students can demonstrate these skills to the class or in conjunction with the exhibit. One resource for this information is the Flag section of the *World Book Encyclopedia*.

3. Students can research semaphore language. Ask them to demonstrate how to spell words or send messages in semaphore.

4. Students can research another method of communication such as sign language. Have children learn a poem or song in sign language.

## Resources

1. United Nations Publications, Room 1059, New York City, New York 10017, 212-963-1234. Contact the United Nations Gift Shop about buying fabric flags of its member nations as well as posters of the United Nations building.

2. If you live in a large urban center such as New York or Los Angeles, local consulates are good sources of posters of people and scenery from different countries. Sometimes, these organizations will also have videos and sample flags available. If such offices exist in your city, you can locate them in the telephone book.

3. Many communities have local cultural groups and organizations that represent residents whose families or ancestors immigrated to the United States. These groups are often devoted to maintaining cultural identity and traditions. Retired members of such groups or persons with flexible working schedules might be willing to come to your school with traditional costumes, folklore, and cultural artifacts to explain life in the country with which they are familiar.

4. The local library is another source of speakers for this table. Although you may not be able to locate any flag experts, your local children's librarian might be able to present a lively storytelling session on folktales from countries of your choice. This is a good way to identify the similarities between people around the world since many of the same folktales are told the world over with different names and animals.

5. Here are some helpful books on flags:

   *Flag: An Eyewitness Book* published by Alfred A. Knopf (1989).

   *Guide to the Flags of the World* by Mauro Talocci, published in the United States by William Morrow and Company (1982).

   *Flags* by David Jeffers, published by Franklin Watts (1985) (contains semaphore system alphabet and international flag alphabet code).

From *Classroom Museums: Touchable Tables for Kids*, published by GoodYear Books. Copyright © 1992 Pamela Marx.

Name_____ Date _____

## Can you create a peace flag?

Think of things that remind you of peace and how to get along with others. These things are symbols of peace. Can you create a flag using these symbols?

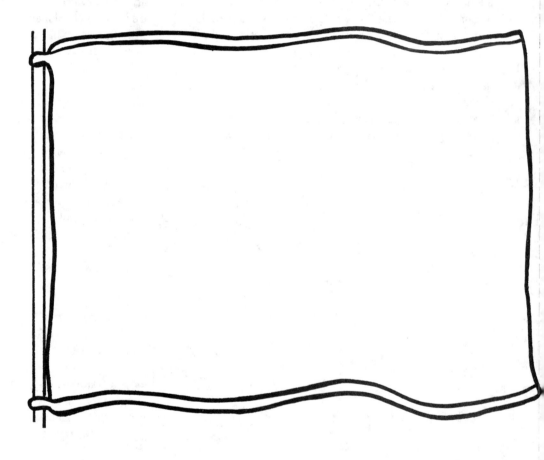

**The United Nations Flag:** This flag is one that symbolizes world peace. It has a light blue background. Its symbols are drawn in white. A white globe is surrounded by olive branches.

From *Classroom Museums: Touchable Tables for Kids*, published by GoodYear Books. Copyright © 1992 Pamela Marx.

Name_____ Date _____

## Make a coat of arms for your family.

Think about your family—the things in which you are interested, the things you like to do together, the talents you have, the sports you enjoy together, the foods you like, and the pets you have. Think about plants, animals, and other symbols for all those things. Draw one symbol in each box of the shield below.

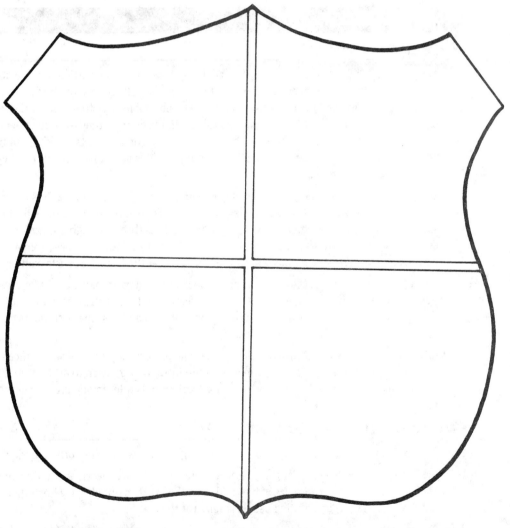

**You have created a coat of arms for your family. You have become part of the tradition of heraldry.**

From *Classroom Museums: Touchable Tables for Kids*, published by GoodYear Books. Copyright © 1992 Pamela Marx.

# Impressionist Painters and Their Art

*This exhibit table introduces students to art appreciation and art history. Impressionism is the focus since many people are familiar with the Impressionists and posters of their art are readily available.*

## Teacher Guidance

### Getting Started

Peruse the table text and the discussion guidelines. As you do, note particularly the discussions of what art is and how color is used. Information about the artists themselves is really secondary. By focusing on what art is, what artists look at when they paint, and how they use colors, this exhibit table, the student activities, and the discussion materials are designed to teach students how to enjoy paintings. If, in addition, they learn how to place the art in its historical context, so much the better. Through the process of collecting artifacts, making exhibit materials, and discussing art posters, children become acquainted with famous paintings and famous painters. They also become aware of the ways in which colors can be experienced and used.

This exhibit works well for all children, kindergarten through eighth grade. It is an opportunity for those up through second grade to look at pictures and talk about what they see. In conjunction with this, the concepts of primary and secondary colors can be explored. With children in grades three through six, explore the pictures themselves in more detail and discuss the artists and complementary colors. Children in grades seven and eight can investigate all these issues, and look also at what was going on in the world at the time the artists painted.

Above all, this exhibit offers an opportunity to look at and start thinking about famous paintings. No answer or statement about a painting is really wrong. Children learn that they each bring something to every painting they see and that they can enjoy them in their own ways. Kindergarten and first-grade students can find many more dinosaurs in Van Gogh's work than he ever intended.

After you have looked over the materials in this chapter, contact the education office at a local art museum. Ask to speak to a docent who can give you tips on how to introduce children to art and what to expect. This can be done by telephone. Art museum docents lead tours for local school children and are very familiar with the kinds of questions they ask.

### Curriculum Integration

The following may give you a few ideas for incorporating art discussions into other curriculum areas.

1. **Art History:** Using the familiar turf of Impressionist art, children learn about Vincent van Gogh, Claude Monet, and Mary Cassatt. They see examples of how and what the artists painted. They learn that, while we appreciate these artists today, when they began painting people laughed at them.

2. **Art:** Introducing Impressionist art gives rise to classroom art opportunities for children to try to see the world as the Impressionists did. The Impressionists did not paint each leaf on a tree. They painted splashes of color that they saw reflected in the bright sunlight. For younger children, this table is a great jumping-off point for exploring primary and secondary colors and how they mix and change. For older children, it is a chance to explore different ways to create pictures and the concept of complementary colors.

From *Classroom Museums: Touchable Tables for Kids,* published by GoodYear Books. Copyright © 1992 Pamela Marx.

3. **World Geography:** Discuss Impressionist art and artists in conjunction with a world map. The Impressionist movement began in France. Mary Cassatt was a famous Impressionist artist who was originally from the United States but moved to Europe. Paul Gauguin moved to Tahiti to work on his art. Vincent van Gogh came from Holland. Reinforce your geography lessons using this technique.

4. **World History:** The Impressionists painted during a period of relative peace in Europe, shortly after the beginning of the Industrial Revolution. They painted with beautiful, striking colors. They repeatedly painted scenes in nature or of city people visiting the countryside. Why was this so? In the dawn of the industrial age, did people long for the peace of the countryside? Even then, did they look back wistfully at the "good old days"? Did the absence of war allow them to focus on life's pleasures, rather than its pains?

## *Table Appearance*

*This exhibit is one of the easiest to prepare, since tabletop materials are optional. Cover your wall with at least six art posters. If you use a table exhibit, it might look like this.*

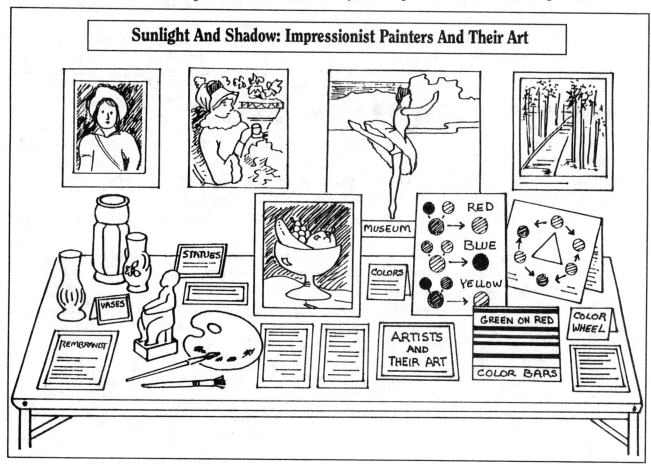

1. Place a collection of small painted vases, carved wooden statues or dishes, glazed clay sculptures (some of these can be student work), and mosaics on the table. This assortment of *colloquial,* or folk, art represents the kind of art the children live with every day. Much of it can come from their homes. Try to include examples from other countries.

2. Fill the middle section of the table with small art prints. Eight-by-ten-inch prints are inexpensive and can be mounted with posterboard triangles on the backs so that they stand upright on your exhibit table. Try to display prints that illustrate traditional styles of art before the Impressionists as well as some Cubist or other Post-Impressionist works. It is interesting to compare these pictures with the Impressionists' work. Such comparisons help children see how ideas about art change.

3. Spread large versions of the Activity Sheet charts in this chapter over the last section of the table. If you make up both charts, you will have a primary/secondary color chart and a complementary color chart. You can also include a

From *Classroom Museums: Touchable Tables for Kids,* published by GoodYear Books. Copyright © 1992 Pamela Marx.

complementary color experiment board here. (See the first student activity suggested later in this chapter.) Make sure you mount these charts on posterboard triangles so that they stand upright on your table.

4.  Photocopy the table text, cut it apart, and display the section called "What is Art?" in front of your collected artifacts. The text relating to the Impressionists accompanies your small prints. "How Artists Use Color" explains the color charts.

5.  You might forego the table and mount the text on construction paper. Intersperse the text with your art posters. This display might be suitable as a long-term exhibit on an otherwise vacant wall.

6.  Gummy adhesives work well to mount your art posters for wall display. Attach adhesive to at least twelve points on large posters. Press firmly onto wall.

## Sample Touchables

Art posters are the most important materials for this exhibit. They are the focus for student discussion. Through donations and inexpensive purchases you should be able to collect a nice cross-section of portraits, still lifes, and landscapes. Try to gather at least six wall-sized posters.

Consider using artists' supplies as touchables. Some children have never seen such things as palettes, canvases, artists' paints, and brushes. You may be able to borrow some from local amateur artists. Place them in the exhibit near your art artifacts.

For other possible touchables, see the section of this chapter entitled Table Appearance.

## Student Involvement in Table Preparation

Encourage students to become involved in the preparation of this exhibit by bringing in touchables and by creating charts and color experiments.

1.  Ask children to bring samples of wood carvings, painted vases, mosaics, and sculptures from home. These can be items that they have made themselves or that they or their families have collected.

2.  Have some children visited an art museum? Do they have small art prints at home? Encourage them to bring these items for the exhibit.

3.  Middle- and upper-grade children can prepare color charts for the table. By tracing and cutting circles of colored construction paper, they can make very effective informational color charts using the formats suggested on this chapter's activity sheets.

4.  Have children make a complementary color experiment board. Instructions are provided in the Student Activities section of this chapter.

From *Classroom Museums: Touchable Tables for Kids*, published by GoodYear Books. Copyright © 1992 Pamela Marx.

One portion of this text includes brief descriptions of a variety of Impressionist artists. As you collect posters, you can never be sure which artist's work you will come across at a reasonable price. Brief descriptions of several women artists are included. Make an effort to collect art by women.

**Impressionism**

## Sunlight and Shadow: Impressionist Painters and Their Art

## What Is Art?

Throughout history, people have recorded events, shown emotions, and reflected life artistically. They wove designs into baskets. They shaped clays. They carved wood and stone. They painted vases. They painted scenes, people, and places on canvases and hung their paintings on walls.

### Let's Think About Painting.

When you see a painting, what is the first thing that catches your eye? Do you look at the color? Do you look at the subject of the painting—that is, what the artist was painting a picture of? Artists paint pictures of many different things. They paint people. They paint trees. They paint fruit. Sometimes they just paint a feeling.

Pictures of one or a few people are called *portraits*. In a portrait, the artist focuses on people. Sometimes people pay the artist to paint a picture of them. Sometimes the artist just likes the way the people look so he or she paints a picture of them. The artist wants to show something about them.

Sometimes an artist picks a few objects to paint. Have you ever seen a painting of a bowl of fruit or a vase of flowers? These pictures are called *still life* paintings. Why do you think they are called still lifes?

Some paintings are of big outdoor scenes. The artist takes a big outdoor scene of trees or fields or roads or buildings and paints it onto a canvas. Pictures like this are called *landscapes*.

When you look at the history of painting, you see that portraits, landscapes, and still lifes have been painted in many different styles. Sometimes painters painted a scene exactly the way it looked. The painting looked like a huge photograph of the thing painted. Sometimes painters used stylized methods. The object painted looked longer or rounder than it really was. Sometimes painters focused on certain aspects of what they saw. For example, they focused on how light struck the object they painted.

From *Classroom Museums: Touchable Tables for Kids*, published by GoodYear Books. Copyright © 1992 Pamela Marx.

Impressionists

# The Artists Called Impressionists

One group of painters who painted a little over a hundred years ago came to be called the Impressionists. Their style of painting shocked many people. Some people thought their pictures were not finished. Some people thought their pictures looked too wild. Some people thought their pictures looked strange. Their painted flowers did not look like real flowers.

Today, the Impressionists are considered very great artists by most people. They showed us a new way of looking at things. The Impressionists used bolder colors and thicker brush strokes than painters before them. They tried to capture the way the light looked.

Edouard Manet led the way for the Impressionists in the 1860s. If he painted a tree, he used dabs of color to show what he saw as he looked at it. He did not paint the individual leaves. If you look at the painting up close, it just looks like spots of color. Yet, if you look at the painting from a distance, you see a wonderful tree.

Try an experiment with your own eyes. Pretend you are an Impressionist painter. Look quickly at a tree or a garden of flowers from a distance in the bright sunlight. Do you see each leaf? Do you see each petal? Or do you see a splash of color? The Impressionists painted these splashes of color.

Many artists painted in this style until the 1890s. A man named Claude Monet became the most famous. When he started painting, he had no money and sold his paintings for a few dollars each. But he was committed to painting. He especially liked to paint outdoor scenes. He loved to paint nature and scenes from the vast gardens around his home. Over the years he also became more interested in painting scenes in series. He would paint a haystack or a church or water lilies over and over again at different times of the day and year. In this way, he showed how his subject looked in different sunlight and seasons.

There are many other famous Impressionist painters. Have you heard of some of them?

## Mary Cassatt

A famous Impressionist painter from America was a woman named Mary Cassatt. While she painted a variety of different subjects, many of her paintings depicted women and their children. She knew from the time she was young that she wanted to be a painter when she grew up.

## Camille Pissarro

Pissarro was a leading Impressionist painter and teacher. In the 1880s, he had many followers and students. He liked to paint scenes of nature and the outdoors. He was also one of the few leading Impressionists to recognize the value and importance of artists with painting styles different from his own. Some of the artists Pissarro thought had talent included Edgar Degas, Vincent van Gogh, Paul Gauguin, and Georges Seurat.

## Alfred Sisley

Sisley came from a wealthy family and, until 1870, painted only as a hobby. Then, his family began to have financial trouble. As a result, he decided to make painting a career. He hoped to earn a living at it. He often painted in subdued tones.

## Berthe Morisot

Morisot was a French woman who achieved fame as an Impressionist painter. She was born in 1841 and died in 1895. She organized the last group exhibition of Impressionist work.

From *Classroom Museums: Touchable Tables for Kids*, published by GoodYear Books. Copyright © 1992 Pamela Marx.

## Edgar Degas

Degas was a French painter. He was born in 1834. He painted many studies of ballet dancers at dance and practice. Mary Cassatt was one of his students.

## Auguste Renoir

Born in 1841, Renoir became a famous Impressionist painter. He painted many scenes of French city dwellers, both as portraits and on outings in the country.

# Impressionists

# Beyond Impressionism

*As Impressionist painting developed, several key artists moved in different and unique directions. They pushed the use of color in ways not tried by earlier artists.*

## Paul Cezanne

Cezanne was the son of a wealthy French banker. He wanted to be a great Impressionist painter but he also wanted to make changes in the style. He thought his changes would improve his paintings. He believed the lines of Impressionist painting to be too soft and the subjects shapeless. Cezanne used patches of color to create paintings with bolder patterns and shapes.

## Vincent van Gogh

Van Gogh was a Dutch painter. He led a very troubled life. He loved painting but the public did not understand his work and he sold very few paintings. Van Gogh used very bold brush strokes. In his later paintings, his brush strokes were often large and twisted. He painted with strong, exciting colors. He painted scenes of common people, farms, and rural villages.

## Paul Gauguin

Gauguin was a Frenchman who began to work in business but was drawn to painting. As he learned more about being a painter, he decided he must change his lifestyle. He wanted to live a simpler life. To do this, he moved to the island of Tahiti. Patterns of color and design were very important to Gauguin. He often painted scenes of the people in Tahiti.

## Georges Seurat

Seurat died when he was only thirty-two but his method of painting was unique. He was interested in light and how it broke down into colors. He painted with tiny circles or points of color. Painters who adopted his style were called *pointillists*.

From *Classroom Museums: Touchable Tables for Kids*, published by GoodYear Books. Copyright © 1992 Pamela Marx.

## How Artists Use Color

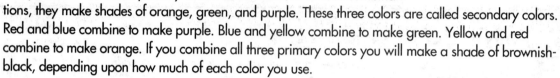

*Painters usually work from a palette of colors. They mix a few basic colors to get the shades they need for their painting.*

### What Are Primary and Secondary Colors?

The three primary colors from which other colors are made are red, blue, and yellow. When these primary colors are blended in various combinations, they make shades of orange, green, and purple. These three colors are called secondary colors. Red and blue combine to make purple. Blue and yellow combine to make green. Yellow and red combine to make orange. If you combine all three primary colors you will make a shade of brownish-black, depending upon how much of each color you use.

Sometimes the Impressionists did not mix their colors on the palette. (A *palette* is a thin board on which a painter places and mixes colors.) They would take dabs of several colors and apply them directly to their canvases. If they wanted to make a color look particularly bright, they would apply that color next to its complementary color.

### What Is a Complementary Color?

A complementary color exists for every primary color. To find out the complementary color for yellow, mix together the remaining two primary colors (red and blue) to make purple. The complementary color for red is green (the combination of blue and yellow). The complementary color for blue is orange (the combination of red and yellow). When red is used next to its complementary color, green, both colors look brighter than they would next to other colors.

If an artist does not want a color to look bright, would he or she use it next to its complementary color? No, the artist would use the color next to some other color.

From *Classroom Museums: Touchable Tables for Kids*, published by GoodYear Books. Copyright © 1992 Pamela Marx.

Impressionist Painters and Their Art

**Teacher Resources**

## Discussion Guidelines

*Have exhibit speakers or teachers use these discussion guidelines to help children explore and enjoy the art posters in your exhibit.*

1.  What is art and why do people paint?
    What do you think art is?

    | | |
    |---|---|
    | *Painting* | *Molding clay* |
    | *Carving* | *Collage making* |
    | *Mosaic making* | *Crayon or pencil drawing* |

    Are the paintings and statues in museums different from other paintings and statues? If so, how are they different?

    Likely answers from children are:

    > *They are special or unique.*
    > *They are better than others.*
    > *They are older.*
    > *They are made by famous people.*

    Other possible answers:

    > *They are good examples of a particular style of painting or sculpture.*
    > *They are artworks that once graced famous buildings or churches.*

    Why do people paint?

    > *To relax*
    > *To play with the colors*
    > *To make something pretty*
    > *To make money*

    With what tools do painters paint?

    | | | |
    |---|---|---|
    | *Brushes* | *Canvases* | *Watercolors* |
    | *Oils* | *Acrylics* | *Charcoal* |

    What do painters paint?

    | | |
    |---|---|
    | *Landscapes* | *Portraits* |
    | *Still lifes* | *City scenes* |

    When you look at a painting, can you tell what the artist was interested in when he or she painted it?

    Look at a landscape with people in it. The people will typically be small.

    > *Can you tell how the people feel?*
    > *Are they happy or sad?*
    > *Are they tired? Are they young or old?*

    Usually it is hard to answer these questions from a landscape because the artist was more interested in the natural setting than the people.

    Now look at the landscape again. What can you tell from the picture?

    > *What season of the year is it?*
    > *Is it hot or cold?*
    > *Is it stormy or sunny?*
    > *Is it a picture of farmland, city buildings, or fields of flowers?*

    Now look at a picture of people. There are two kinds. One is a portrait where you see one or a few people up close. Another is a study of people in action—at work or play. What can you tell about people in a portrait?

    > *Can you tell how they feel?*
    > *Are they young or old?*
    > *Why do you think they wanted to have their pictures painted?*
    > *Are they wealthy or are they working people?*

2.  Artistic styles change over time. How were the Impressionists special?

    During some periods of history, portraits were painted mostly for people who commissioned them. This means they paid to have their pictures painted. In the last hundred years, more portraits have been painted of people just because artists found these people interesting, not because they could pay for the picture.

    Over the years, styles of painting have changed. Big changes occurred more than a century ago when the Impressionists developed their style.

    How did people react to their work?

    > *People were shocked.*
    > *People laughed at them.*
    > *People thought the paintings were not finished.*

    But the Impressionists were experimenting.

    When you paint, do you like to try new things?

    Do you like to see what happens when you mix colors together?

    Do you like to see how it will look if you try to paint a shadow with one color rather than another?

    Painters are like this too. The Impressionists experimented with a whole new way of seeing.

*From Classroom Museums: Touchable Tables for Kids,* published by GoodYear Books. Copyright © 1992 Pamela Marx.

Impressionists were fascinated with how light affected the things they painted.

**Discussion leader's note:** You might want to explain the differences in style by trying the following. You will need two still-life or flower posters. One should be an Impressionist work by an artist like Cezanne or Monet. The other should be more classical in style, perhaps by Jan Davidsz de Heem or another painter from an earlier period such as the 17th Century. Block out all but a three-by-three-inch square on each of the two paintings. Point to the classical painting and the flower visible in the unblocked area. Ask the students to tell you what they see. What has the artist painted a picture of? They should be able to easily identify it as a flower.

*Can they see the stem?*
*Can they see the petals?*
*Can they see the stamen?*

Now, point to the unblocked patch in the Impressionist painting. It should look like a patch of rough color. Can the children tell what it is, or does it just look like color?

Take away the covering paper. Can everyone tell that the splotch of color is really a flower? How can you tell?

*Can you see the petals?*
*Can you see the stem?*
*Can you see the stamen?*

When the Impressionist painted this flower, what was he (or she) interested in?

*The structure of the flower?*
*The individual petals?*
*The veins on the leaves?*

What does he show you about the flower?

*Color          Shape          Lighting*
Ask these same questions about the classical painting.

3.    Besides the subject of a painting (the thing painted), what else can you look for in a painting?

### Perspective

What other things can you see in a painting?

Have you heard about something called *perspective?*

What is perspective?

Let's assume the artist is painting a flower.

*(Note: Use as your subject example any object in one of the posters you have in your exhibit. It need not be a flower. This is by way of example only.)*

When the artist looked at the flower to paint it, was he (or she) looking straight at the flower?

Was he (or she) looking down on the flower?

Was he (or she) looking up at the flower?

### Light

From which direction is light coming?

*Front          Back          Side*
How can you tell?

*Shadows*
*Light in one part of picture—one corner or to the side*

### Color

Painters often start with very basic colors and then mix them on a palette until they make the colors they want to use. What do you know about colors?

Do you know what primary colors are?

*Red          Yellow          Blue*
When you mix primary colors, what happens?

How do you make orange?

*Mix red and yellow.*
How do you make green?

*Mix yellow and blue.*
How do you make purple?

*Mix red and blue.*
Painters know a lot about colors and how to mix them.

Impressionists and those who followed them also experimented more with new ways to use colors. They often painted with larger strokes. Sometimes they would not mix paint on the palette but would put two or more different colors side by side on the brush and then apply the paint to the canvas. This resulted in a new effect.

The Impressionists often used complementary colors to make other colors look even more dramatic.

What is a complementary color?

*Take the primary color red. You make its complementary color by mixing the remaining two primary colors (yellow and blue) to make green.*
What is the complementary color for yellow?

*Purple.*
What is the complementary color for blue?

*Orange.*

## Student Activities

1.    Let children make their own complementary color "experiments." Give each child a sheet of construction paper in the primary color of his or her choosing. Then, instruct students to cut three-eights-inch strips of construction paper in three other colors, one of them being the color complementary to the primary color they chose. They should cut six or seven strips of each color. Paste the strips onto the primary colors so that one-quarter to three-eights-inch of primary color shows between each pasted strip. For example, assume red is the

From *Classroom Museums: Touchable Tables for Kids,* published by GoodYear Books. Copyright © 1992 Pamela Marx.

primary color and the child has cut strips of orange, purple, and green (red's complementary color). On the top third of the paper, he or she should glue the orange strips with red showing between each. On the middle third, glue the purple strips with red showing between each. On the bottom third, glue the green strips with red showing through. When you look at the completed chart, the red should look brightest where the strips of its complementary color, green, are glued.

2. Have students make their own painting palettes from cardboard and waxed paper. Staple several layers of waxed paper on a small piece of cardboard. On the top sheet of waxed paper, children place one dab of each primary color. Then they experiment with mixing their own secondary colors and applying them to paper. When the experiment is over, tear off the soiled sheet of waxed paper and you have a clean palette available for a later art experience.

3. Purchase sheets of pre-tinted acetate at a local art store and have children make their own color wheels. For each child, cut three ovals of acetate approximately two by three inches in size—one blue, one yellow, one red. Punch a hole in the bottom of each of the three pieces of acetate and fasten with a brad. Holding their color wheels up to the light, children can overlay the colors and discover secondary colors.

4. Another way for children to experiment with primary colors is to have a playdough day. Ask parents to make playdough. You need two batches each of red, blue, and yellow. Each child gets a ball of each of the three colors to mix and match.

## PLAYDOUGH

A good playdough recipe is: 2 cups white flour; ½ cup salt; 4 tablespoons cream of tartar; 2 cups water; 2 tablespoons vegetable oil; 4 teaspoons food coloring. Combine all ingredients except food coloring. Cook in a saucepan over medium heat, stirring constantly. It takes four to five minutes. Just when you think it will never get done, it pulls away from the sides of the pan to form a large mass in the middle of the pan. Let it cool. Work in food coloring until you get the desired color. When it is *completely* cool, seal it in a plastic bag.

5. Give older children time to sit under a tree or on the grass and sketch the shapes they see with markers or paint. Each should pick an object (tree, flower, bush, or wall) and paint its shapes. Ask them *not* to outline first and then color in. Tell them to try to use splotches of color to re-create on paper the object they choose to draw.

## Resources

1. In your effort to gather art posters and prints, start first with your school. Do any of the teachers have samples they will lend? Then check with local museums. While smaller museums seldom have the resources to make outright donations, they often have sale or low-priced posters. If you tell them how you plan to use the posters, they might offer you their member discount. Local art museums may also have teacher education nights at which they sell art posters for a fraction of the ordinary cost to the public.

2. Some of the major museums in large urban centers may make limited donations upon request, whether in writing or by telephone. The Metropolitan Museum of Art in New York is one you might try:
The Metropolitan Museum of Art
Fifth Avenue at 82nd Street
New York, New York 10028
212-879-5500
A good source of museum listings is found in *The New York Public Library Desk Reference,* a Stonesong Press Book published by Webster's New World.

3. There are several places you can go to find speakers for your art table. One source is the art and art history departments of a local college. Any local art collective might be able to help. Quite often these groups are made up of local artists who either have flexible work schedules or are retired. Many of these groups are anxious to engage in community service and to foster an appreciation of the artistic process among young people. Sometimes they will request a nominal fee.

Another source for speakers is your local art museum. Docents are well trained and informative. The museum may have a formal outreach program or may be able to put you in touch with docents who will volunteer at your school.

From *Classroom Museums: Touchable Tables for Kids,* published by GoodYear Books. Copyright © 1992 Pamela Marx.

Name_____ Date _____

## Primary and Secondary Color Chart

What are the three primary colors?  There are also three secondary colors.  What are they? **Color this chart as shown.**

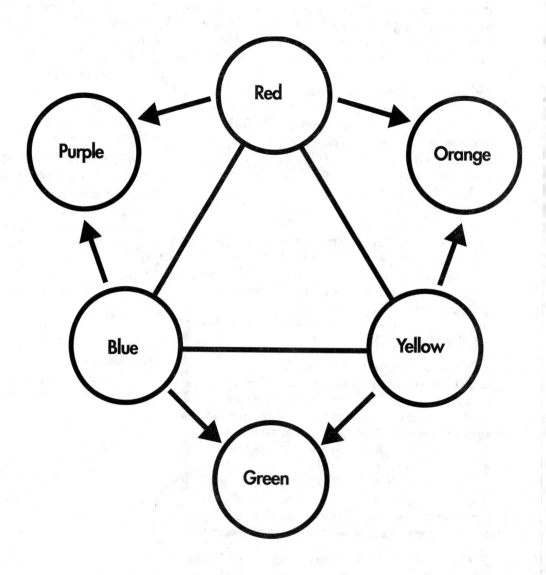

How do you make a secondary color?

From *Classroom Museums: Touchable Tables for Kids*, published by GoodYear Books. Copyright © 1992 Pamela Marx.

Impressionist Painters and Their Art

Colors II

## Complementary Color Chart

What is a complementary color? Can you tell from this chart?
**Color this chart as shown.**

Red    Yellow

Orange      complements      Blue

Yellow    Blue

Green      complements      Red

Blue    Red

Purple      complements      Yellow

From *Classroom Museums: Touchable Tables for Kids*, published by GoodYear Books. Copyright © 1992 Pamela Marx.

# Winter Festivals Around the World

*This exhibit gives children an understanding of the bonds that unite all people. Through celebrations and festivals, people express their joys, needs, and fears. These emotions are common to all people. As we learn that the celebrations of people around the world have similar origins and meet common needs, we enhance cultural awareness and understanding.*

## Teacher Guidance

### Getting Started

This chapter provides opportunities for children to learn about celebrations around the world and to analyze their own practices. Through this analysis, they begin to see the relationship between their own family traditions and those of people in other countries.

To become familiar with this subject matter, review the table text. It touches on winter festivals including Christmas, Hanukkah, and new year and harvest holidays. Once familiar with the territory, survey your students and school community to determine what holiday traditions exist in families in your school. Can some of these families share touchables with the exhibit? Can some of them demonstrate traditions or food preparation? Let the demographic makeup of your community guide the direction and focus of your exhibit.

Once you decide upon the focus of your exhibit, visit the children's section of your local library. You'll probably find a good selection of books about festivals and customs from all over the world. This research will give you more in-depth information about particular holidays you want your exhibit to cover.

### Curriculum Integration

You can integrate this exhibit into your curriculum in several ways.

1. **Geography:** The festivals and customs covered in this chapter come from, among other places, Europe, Asia, Central America, and India. This diversity of study allows you to incorporate world geography issues into class work.

2. **Multicultural Studies:** Since the exhibit focuses primarily on people and the things they do to celebrate, this chapter is ideal for use in a multicultural awareness curriculum. Children learn about different kinds of foods people eat, the various kinds of arts and crafts people make and use, and the similarity in celebrations the world over.

3. **Cooking:** This chapter is a perfect opportunity to undertake a month-long cooking curriculum. Each week, children can make and sample foods from a different country.

From *Classroom Museums: Touchable Tables for Kids*, published by GoodYear Books. Copyright © 1992 Pamela Marx.

# Table Appearance

*Based upon the demographics of your local community, you may decide to make a particular holiday the focal point of the exhibit. This is especially true if you have a speaker who knows one holiday especially well, or who can present folktales from a particular country.*

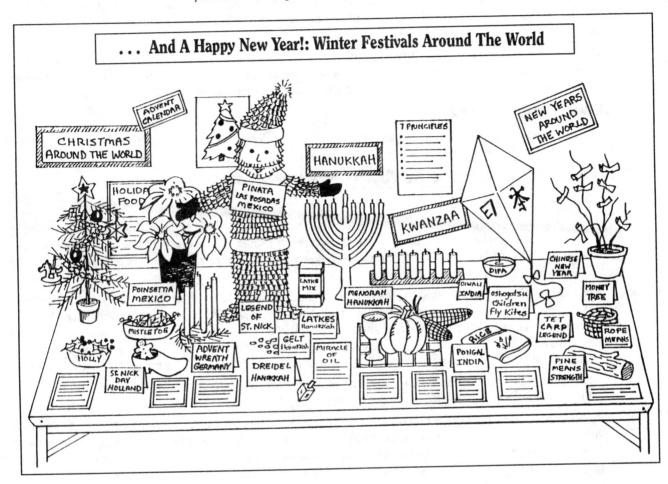

... And A Happy New Year!: Winter Festivals Around The World

The organization of the exhibit suggested here assumes that you choose Christmas as the focal point of your exhibit. But you may choose to focus on another holiday. Remember that the table should enhance cultural awareness. Accordingly, while your exhibit may focus on a particular holiday, try to include information, drawings, and touchables related to several different holidays and traditions.

Place relevant table text on the viewing side of the table. Arrange touchables as suggested here.

1. **Christmas:** A small tree with Christmas decorations that represent different parts of the world can be the centerpiece of the Christmas display. These ornaments can include woven straw, carved wooden toys, a fake spider web, decorated egg shapes, and strung popcorn and/or cranberries, nuts, or fruit. Stay away from the glass balls and tinsel that are very common and also likely to break or make a mess.

    Place traditional holiday plants on the table, including poinsettias, mistletoe, holly, rosemary, and ivy.

    Look for several used or inexpensive Advent calendars to hang on the wall. Place a wreath on the table with four candles standing in it to represent an Advent wreath.

    Fill a wooden shoe with candy to help children visualize the Dutch celebration of St. Nicholas Day. Perhaps some children make gingerbread houses at home. Include and discuss these as examples of traditional foods and food crafts.

    A piñata on the table will generate discussion about the Mexican tradition of Las Posadas.

From *Classroom Museums: Touchable Tables for Kids*, published by GoodYear Books. Copyright © 1992 Pamela Marx.

2. **Hanukkah:** To represent the Jewish Festival of Lights, place a menorah with candles on the table. Surround it with several plastic dreidels, nuts, and gold-covered chocolate coins (Hanukkah *gelt*). If you don't have a menorah or dreidel, children can make them out of clay. See the Resources section of this chapter for books that provide directions for these projects.

3. **Harvest Festivals:** Pumpkins, baskets, and harvest foods can represent the African-American Kwanzaa celebration. Make a "Kwanzaa table," including seven candles, the unity cup, baskets, an ear of corn, and a small straw mat such as a placemat. Pongal is the Indian rice harvest festival. Any artifacts from India along with Indian rice make good touchables.

4. **New Year Celebrations:** Sample touchables for this section of the table include a money tree holding coins and candy wrapped in red tissue paper, paper money, Chinese or Japanese dolls, and carp or fish windsocks and kites. Rope, pine, and bamboo can also grace the table to represent the Japanese New Year and the legend of the Sun Goddess.

## Sample Touchables

Suggestions for the touchables for this exhibit are made in the preceding section entitled Table Appearance. Feel free to include as well representations of American Thanksgiving and traditional American New Year festivities.

## Student Involvement in Table Preparation

Student involvement in the preparation of this table can take several different forms.

1. Children can share holiday decorations they have at home that reflect a tradition or decorating style unique to some part of the world. These can be tree decorations, lanterns, pictures, or manger scenes. (Before using any overtly religious material, check local school regulations. This exhibit is designed to avoid such references except as they directly relate to a cultural festival or celebration.)

2. Have children make a *piñata* to illustrate the Las Posadas celebration of Mexico. Many instructions are available to teachers for making real *piñatas*. The simplest method is to blow up a large balloon and cover it with papier-mâché made from strips of newspaper dipped in starch or glue and water. When the form is complete and dry, glue on fringed strips of crepe or tissue paper until the entire surface is covered. Add a face or other design with construction paper. Children might enjoy filling the *piñata* with candy and breaking it during a class party (after the exhibit is finished, of course).

3. Children can make an Advent calendar to display on an exhibit wall. This calendar might be a larger version of the one included in the activity sheets at the end of this chapter.

4. Children can make *parols,* or Filipino Christmas stars, to decorate the exhibit area. Trace and cut large star shapes on posterboard or stiff dinner-sized paper or foam plates. Then, cut out the interior of the stars, leaving star-shaped frames. Have the children trace the outside outlines of the stars onto tissue using these stencils and cut the tissue stars out. Glue the tissues to the star frames. The completed *parols* can be taped to dowels or paper towel rolls for carrying (as in a parade), or they can be hung from the ceiling. In an easier version, cut the star from the paper plate or posterboard (do not cut out the interior to create a frame) and cover the star with bits of colored tissue and foil paper.

5. Have children create a money tree as a touchable representing the Chinese New Year. Cover an old coffee can with orange, red, or gold paper. Fill it with plaster and insert a large branch. Cover the branch with paper flowers and pennies or candy wrapped in red tissue.

6. Have children help arrange touchables on the exhibit table.

7. This exhibit lends itself well to student presentations. Assign students research topics such as Hanukkah, Chinese New Year, Tet Festival, Kwanzaa, Christmas in Italy, or Las Posadas. Students might present their findings to other classes when they come to see the exhibit. Or, reports can focus on the history of particular holiday symbols such as the Christmas tree, the poinsettia, or the Advent calendar. Oral presentations should include a few short holiday legends. Examples can be found in many books. Some of the legends referred to in the table text here are those of Befana, St. Nicholas, the first Christmas tree, the silver spider web, the Vietnamese Kitchen God, and the Japanese Sun Goddess.

From *Classroom Museums: Touchable Tables for Kids*, published by GoodYear Books. Copyright © 1992 Pamela Marx.

## Table Text

*This table text provides information about a variety of winter holidays. Use the resource books listed at the end of this chapter and other books available at local libraries to provide information about other holidays you would like to cover. Delete any holidays that are not appropriate. Finally, feel free to add touchables and tags about traditional American Thanksgiving and new year celebrations.*

## Christmas

### ... And a Happy New Year! Winter Festivals Around the World

People have long celebrated the changes of season. Since ancient times in cultures around the world, spring, fall, harvest time, and winter have given rise to celebration. In this exhibit, we will explore winter festivals around the world.

In ancient times, many celebrations centered around the harvest—giving thanks for food, warding off droughts, celebrating the sun. During some times of the year, the days are long. During other times, the days grow short. Ancient peoples knew these cycles but believed them to be mysterious. As a result, in late December, when the days begin to get longer again, ancient people celebrated the much needed "return" of the sun. It was a time of relaxation and feasting, lighting fires, and praising the new sun. It was a celebration of the new life the sun would bring in the spring.

Some of the winter holidays celebrated around the world are Christmas, harvest festivals, new year celebrations, and Hanukkah. Let's find out about them.

## Christmas

The celebration of Christmas occurs around the world. Among Christians, it is the time to mark the birth of Jesus Christ. For others, it is a holiday that has come to represent peace on earth and a time to be together. People who celebrate Christmas do so with lights, decorations, food, and parades. These traditions vary from country to country. In the United States, people who celebrate Christmas have adopted many customs that were brought by immigrants from their native lands.

## Christmas Tree

This is perhaps the most popular Christmas tradition. The Christmas tree is not just used in Western countries. Some people in Japan have adopted the custom as well.

Several stories surround the tree's early use in Germany. In the Middle Ages, many Germans celebrated the feast of Adam and Eve. They decked fir trees with apples to commemorate the tree of knowledge in plays and rituals. On Christmas, they burned candelabra of lights called *lightstocks*. Over the years, people added the lightstocks to the tree, and the Christmas tree was born.

A legend about the very first Christmas tree says that a famous German minister named Martin Luther looked up one night at the starlight flickering through the trees of the forest. He was so impressed by the beautiful sight that he cut a tree, took it home, and filled it with candles.

Whoever had the idea for the first tree, it certainly became a popular one. The tradition soon spread through the Scandinavian countries, then to the rest of Europe and America, and on to much of the world.

From *Classroom Museums: Touchable Tables for Kids*, published by GoodYear Books. Copyright © 1992 Pamela Marx.

## Ornaments

*You can see the influence of many countries in the decorations people place on their Christmas trees. Some foreign customs are now common in America. Some are not. Which kinds of decorations have you seen on Christmas trees?*

### Ornaments **Stars and Birds**

In Poland, straw stars and birds are popular tree decorations.

### Ornaments **Wooden or Straw Animals or People**

In Sweden, decorations made of straw and small carved wooden toys are popular.
In Lithuania, straw shapes and bird ornaments are a sign of good crops for the coming year.

### Ornaments **Pickle**

In Germany, a pickle is hidden on the tree. The first child to find it wins a special present. Can you find the pickle on the tree?

### Ornaments **Painted Eggs**

In Czechoslovakia, people etch and paint intricate geometric designs on emptied eggshells.

### Ornaments **Spider Web**

Some Ukrainians place a spider and web on the tree for good luck. According to legend, an old woman too poor to decorate her tree woke up on Christmas morning to find its branches covered with spider webs turned to silver.

### Ornaments **Origami**

Origami is the Japanese art of folding paper. In recent years, this traditional art has been adapted for the Christmas tree. Paper animals, boxes, and angels hang from tree branches. Christmas trees in Japan are often covered with tiny fans and paper lanterns.

### Ornaments **Popcorn and Cranberries**

The first Christmas trees in America were decorated simply, with paper chains and stars and strings of cranberries and popcorn. Sometimes apples, oranges, and nuts also graced early trees.

## Other Holiday Greenery

*In addition to the Christmas tree, other plants represent the Christmas holiday season to many people.*

### Other Holiday Greenery **Poinsettia**

The poinsettia is a beautiful red-leaved plant that blooms in December. The red part of the plant is its leaf and the small yellow buds at the center of the plant are its flower. It grows well in Mexico and was introduced into the United States by Dr. Joel Poinsett, America's first ambassador to Mexico. He brought the plant home with him from Mexico over a hundred years ago. It became a very popular holiday plant and bears his name.

From *Classroom Museums: Touchable Tables for Kids*, published by GoodYear Books. Copyright © 1992 Pamela Marx.

### Other Holiday Greenery **Mistletoe**

Ancient druids in the British Isles used mistletoe to protect houses from lightning and to drive away evil spirits. The English used it to bring good fortune. Today, the use of mistletoe at Christmas is most popular in America and England. The tradition of kissing under it may symbolize the peace-making spirit of the season.

### Other Holiday Greenery **Holly**

Holly has long been associated with Christmas lore. With its red berries and green leaves, it is often seen in holiday decoration. Holly was used as a tea by some Native Americans who believed it had medicinal powers. Holly also stands for good luck.

### Other Holiday Greenery **Rosemary**

This plant is no longer as popular as it was when used to decorate food served at English Christmas feasts.

## Candles and Lights

*Lights have long been a part of all winter celebrations, including Christmas. Centuries before the celebration of Christmas, torches and bonfires were lighted in late December to celebrate the solstice, the shortest day of the year. The beginning of longer days signaled the sun's victory over the spirits of frost and snow and meant new growth and new life were on their way.*

*People use candles in specific ways in different countries around the world. Some of these customs are:*

### Candles and Lights **Philippines**

A Filipino tradition is the *parol,* or Christmas star. Stars of all sizes are framed onto bamboo or wooden dowels and decorated with brightly colored papers, foils, doilies, and pom-poms. They decorate homes. People carry them in parades. Some are made into lanterns lighted by electric lights or candles. People carry these lanterns in local Christmas Eve "Parades of the Stars." They make a lively and beautiful scene.

### Candles and Lights **Spain**

On Christmas Eve, families burn a candle above the door.

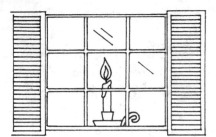

### Candles and Lights **Italy**

People burn candles in windows to light the way for the Christmas child.

### Candles and Lights **Germany/America**

A custom common in several countries is the lighting of one of four candles in an advent wreath on each of the four Sundays preceding Christmas.

From *Classroom Museums: Touchable Tables for Kids,* published by GoodYear Books. Copyright © 1992 Pamela Marx.

## Candles and Lights **Scandinavia**

In the Scandinavian countries people once burned huge logs called *yule logs* during the winter season. While this custom has all but died out, it was very important in years past. People associated it with good luck and bad luck for the coming year. The burning log was believed to drive away evil spirits. If a log stopped burning during the night, it meant bad luck for the year. Some people took ashes from the log and put them under the bed to keep lightning away from the house. The yule log survives today only as a holiday cake which is especially popular in French bakeries.

## Candles and Lights **American Southwest**

The lighting of *luminarias* has spread through the American Southwest. They are very popular in New Mexico. People fill brown paper bags with an inch of sand and a votive or tea candle. They light their *luminarias* on Christmas Eve and line driveways, fences, and the outsides of buildings with them.

## Other Christmas Customs

### Other Christmas Customs **Latin America**

*In Latin American countries, Christmas-related festivities occur between the end of November and January 6. Special days are Nochebuena (or Christmas Eve), which is celebrated by the making of manger scenes, and the Epiphany (or January 6), which celebrates the arrival of the three kings with their gifts in Bethlehem.*

#### Mexico

Las Posadas begins nine days before Christmas. The tradition reenacts Mary's and Joseph's journey to Bethlehem and the baby's birth there. A group of families or friends makes a procession each night, knocking on doors asking for shelter. They are refused until the last door or room when they are allowed to come in and view a prepared nativity scene. A party begins with the *piñata* as its centerpiece, which children take turns trying to break. A *piñata* is a papier-mâché figure that is filled with candy and small presents and hung from the ceiling.

#### Brazil

On Christmas Eve, children put out their shoes for Papa Noel to fill. On Christmas Day, the children search for the gifts Papa Noel hides. They serve their parents a special breakfast. People celebrate with fireworks, boating events, and open-air fiestas.

#### Costa Rica

Climate often dictates the types of decoration used to celebrate a holiday. Costa Rica has a warm, tropical climate. Orchids grow everywhere. People collect them and place them in hollow logs set with lighted candles.

#### Guatemala

Before Christmas in this country, people celebrate El Dia de Guadalupe. The Day of Guadalupe celebrates a story about the vision a small boy once had of the Virgin Mary. Children dress up in costume and parade about. On the ninth day before Christmas, a celebration similar to Las Posadas is held. People carry statues of Joseph and Mary through the streets. The paraders carry *farolitos,* or brightly painted lanterns. They process to houses singing and asking for shelter. They are refused until they announce that they are Mary and Joseph. They are welcomed in and a party begins.

From *Classroom Museums: Touchable Tables for Kids*, published by GoodYear Books. Copyright © 1992 Pamela Marx.

Christmas

## Other Christmas Customs **Europe**

*Many customs and traditions relating to Christmas began in Europe. Some of these traditions spread to the United States. Others remain strictly in the country of their origin. Let's find out about some of the customs and traditions that began in Europe. Which ones have been adopted in the United States by people who celebrate Christmas?*

### England

Sending cards began in England in the 1840s. Since that time, the practice has grown and become very common. Cards are illustrated with all the symbols of Christmas, from Santa Claus to trees, from candy canes to stars.

### Germany

Advent calendars began in Germany and are now popular in America. These pictorial calendars for the month of December contain twenty-four doors, one for each day of the month before Christmas Day. The child opens one paper door each day to reveal a tiny picture. Some Advent calendars now have small pieces of candy or chocolate behind the paper doors.

### Sweden

St. Lucia Day begins the Christmas season in Sweden. St. Lucia is called the Queen of Light. She was a fourth-century Sicilian martyr, and tradition says that she helps Sweden during times of famine. On December 13 each year, the oldest daughter in the family wakes the rest of the household by singing *Santa Lucia* and serving special cakes. She may wear a white dress and a wreath of greenery lighted with candles as a crown upon her head.

### Holland

The time for celebration in this country is December 5 or St. Nicholas Eve. Families gather and give each other surprise gifts. The gifts are hidden or disguised to look like something else. On St. Nicholas Eve, Dutch children put out shoes (traditionally wooden shoes) to be filled with candies and tiny gingerbread cookies left by St. Nick and his helper, Peter. Legend has it that St. Nick rides through the streets on a white horse delivering his gifts.

### Spain

The eve of January 6, or Epiphany, is special for Spanish children. They fill shoes with straw and leave them on a balcony or windowsill. The legend goes that while the camels of the three kings feast on straw, the kings leave gifts to thank the children.

### Italy

As in Spain, holiday gift giving happens in January when Befana, a humble old lady, leaves gifts. The Italian legend says that shepherds told Befana of the birth of a holy baby, but in her search for him she lost sight of the guiding star. She was destined forever to search for the baby leaving presents at each house in case he might be there.

## Other Christmas Customs **North America**

In the United States, Santa Claus brings gifts to children everywhere. He rides in a sleigh from the north pole drawn by eight reindeer and leaves gifts under the tree and in "stockings hung by the chimney with care."

*From Classroom Museums: Touchable Tables for Kids, published by GoodYear Books. Copyright © 1992 Pamela Marx.*

From *Classroom Museums: Touchable Tables for Kids*, published by GoodYear Books. Copyright © 1992 Pamela Marx.

## Hanukkah

A special Jewish holiday called the Festival of Lights, or Hanukkah, centers around the lighting of candles to commemorate a historical and religious event.

Hanukkah commemorates a war in 164 B.C. between the small army of Judah and the Maccabees and the much larger army of King Antiochus. After much fighting over a long time, the Maccabees were victorious. According to legend, after Judah won the final battle, the Jews returned to find their temple ruined. Special oil was required to light the temple lamps. The Jews could only find a tiny bit of the special oil, but it miraculously burned for eight days while new oil was made and blessed. To celebrate this miracle, Hanukkah lasts eight nights. Candles of a nine-candle menorah, or candelabrum, are lighted each night—one the first night, two the second night, and so on. The ninth candle on the menorah is called the shamash, or helper candle. It is used to light the other eight.

On Hanukkah, children play games with a top called a dreidel. They receive gelt, or gold-covered chocolate coins, for prizes. Families feast on latkes, or potato pancakes.

Special stories explain why children play the dreidel game on Hanukkah and why people eat latkes. It is said that, during the years of war, King Antiochus told the Jews they could not worship their god. The Jews gathered together to study their religion despite the king's order. To camouflage the fact that they were studying religion, they played the dreidel game when the king's soldiers came near. People eat latkes at Hanukkah because, during the war, villagers could make them quickly for the soldiers between battles so that they had plenty to eat and kept up their strength.

## New Year Celebrations

### Bahamas

Huge festivals and parades called Junkanoo are held on December 26 and New Year's Eve in these Caribbean islands. People wear beautiful costumes of colorful crepe paper, fancy hats, and unique masks. They play calypso music and dance. A legend says that a Bahaman hero named Johnny Canoe visited the islands each December wearing torn and colorful clothing and a tall hat. When he visited, the people celebrated, and this became Junkanoo.

### China

Sun Nin, the Chinese New Year, is celebrated between mid-January and mid-February. It is the most important Chinese festival and lasts for five days. China is a huge country where millions of people live. Festivities vary from place to place. During the New Year festivities, people exchange gifts. Children give each other oranges and candy. Parents wrap money in red paper and make a money tree for their children. People decorate their homes with red and orange scrolls. The scrolls are inscribed with New Year messages such as "good health, long life, luck, prosperity, and happiness." One well-known New Year greeting is "Gung Hay Fat Choy." It means "Best Wishes and Congratulations." Other symbols of the holiday are apples, oranges, and the color red.

A dragon dance or parade takes place on the third day of the New Year. The head of the dragon is papier-mâché and twelve men act as the dragon's legs. The dragon is thought to bring good luck. Children participate in a lantern procession. The lion dance is another tradition of Chinese New Year. Men and boys dance the lion dance as they parade through the streets.

Each Chinese year has the name of one of twelve animals. The cycle of the animals is completed every twelve years and then begins again.

| 1992 | Year of the Monkey |
|------|---------------------|
| 1993 | Year of the Rooster |
| 1994 | Year of the Dog |
| 1995 | Year of the Boar |
| 1996 | Year of the Rat |
| 1997 | Year of the Ox |
| 1998 | Year of the Tiger |
| 1999 | Year of the Rabbit |
| 2000 | Year of the Dragon |
| 2001 | Year of the Snake |
| 2002 | Year of the Horse |
| 2003 | Year of the Ram/Sheep |
| 2004 | Year of the Monkey |

# New Year's

## Scotland

In Scotland, the new year celebration is the big winter festival called Hogmanay. People celebrate this public holiday with feasting and parties. One custom central to Hogmanay is that of the "first footer." The first person to pass over your doorstep into your house in the new year is said to tell you what kind of luck you will have in the coming year. Spiced ale called *wassail* is served.

## Japan

The important winter festival in Japan is celebrated on the first day of the New Year and is called Oshogatsu. People clean and decorate their houses with rope, bamboo, and pine to represent family ties and long life. Children fly kites. Family and friends get together for feasting. They serve thin buckwheat noodles called *soba*. Hot soup is poured over the noodles. For luck, children try to swallow a long *soba* noodle whole.

Some Japanese still follow a custom of going into the woods a week before the new year to cut down a pine tree. They place the trees by the front doors of their homes to symbolize strength and long life. These are good things for the new year.

A special story goes with the Japanese New Year. It is said that one day the Sun Goddess hid in a large cave. With her retreat into the cave, the world went dark. The other gods and goddesses began to worry. When would the sun come out again? They wanted her to shine. Then they got an idea. They sang and danced outside the cave to coax the Sun Goddess out of her hiding place. Finally the Sun Goddess ventured out of the cave. As she did, the other gods and goddesses quickly threw rope over the opening of the cave so that she could not hide again. This story explains why rope is used to decorate for the holiday. Rope symbolizes hope for a bright new year.

Special pounded rice cakes called *mochi* are also important at this holiday. Some people take mochi cakes of various sizes to shrines and use them for religious ceremonies during the holiday. After these ceremonies, they eat them for good luck and good health.

From *Classroom Museums: Touchable Tables for Kids*, published by GoodYear Books. Copyright © 1992 Pamela Marx.

From *Classroom Museums: Touchable Tables for Kids*, published by GoodYear Books. Copyright © 1992 Pamela Marx.

**New Year's**

## Korea

Sŏlnal, the Korean New Year, is a time for wearing new clothes as well as traditional costumes called *han-pok*. People visit family and friends. A typical New Year greeting is "Please receive many happinesses in the new year." When younger people bow to their elders, the older people respond by giving gifts of fruit and money. *Ttukgook* is a special rice soup cooked for Sŏlnal. Kite-flying is a favorite children's activity.

## Vietnam

In Vietnam, there is a traditional belief that a god protects each household or family. People call it the Kitchen God. This god watches over the family during the year. At each new year, or Tet, he returns to heaven on the back of a large carp to report on the family's doings. Even today, some families acquire a carp before the new year, keep it in a bowl, and release it into a local pond or river on the holiday to help the Kitchen God to heaven.

Another Vietnamese New Year tradition is similar to the Scottish custom of first footers. In Vietnam, the first person to cross your threshold in the new year is said to affect your luck during that year. Families try to arrange to have a friendly face come through the door first. Another tradition is the making and burning of paper money as an offering to ancestors.

The Tet celebration usually occurs as winter changes to spring.

## India

In India, people who follow the Hindu religion celebrate a new year at the beginning of each season. The most spectacular new year celebration is Diwali. Diwali honors the arrival of autumn and occurs in October or November each year. It is a festival of lights. Each home lights *dipas,* small clay bowls filled with oil and wicks, and displays them. They illuminate the night as they decorate doorways and fences. Does this custom remind you of the *luminaria* tradition of the American Southwest?

**St. Nicholas**

## Was There a Real St. Nick?

There really was a man named Nicholas who was designated a saint by the Catholic Church. Born in the fourth century A.D., he was a bishop in the church. Legends tell of his kindness and the miracles he performed. They also tell of his great love of children. He is the patron saint of children and sailors.

Perhaps the most famous legend of his generosity goes like this:

A poor man had three daughters, but no dowries for their marriages. When the first daughter was about to be married, a bag of gold appeared in the man's house one night before the wedding. The daughter had a dowry! When the second daughter was about to be married, another bag of gold appeared in the house one night. When the third daughter was to be married, the man stayed up all night to see who tossed the bags of gold into his house. He caught Nicholas in the act. Nicholas, who liked to do good deeds in secret, begged for anonymity, but word of his generosity leaked out. Soon, when anyone received an unexpected gift, they thanked St. Nicholas.

# Winter Harvest Festivals

## Iroquois

In January, the Iroquois of the northeastern United States celebrate a traditional eight-day Mid-Winter Festival. It is a harvest festival. It begins with the activities of two people called the Big Heads. They dress up and tie scarves or bandannas around their heads. They act as messengers to the community that the festival is beginning. Feasting and ceremonial dances are part of this festival tradition.

## India

In India, harvest time is January. A festival called *Pongal* is held in mid-January to celebrate the rice harvest. It is a time of thanksgiving. Rice from the harvest is cooked in a special ceremony and fed to local cows. The cows are gaily painted or decorated for the festival.

## African-American

*Kwanzaa* is an African-American harvest festival that takes place between December 26 and January 1. *Kwanzaa* is the Swahili word for "first fruits," as in first fruits of the harvest. People celebrate the holiday with parades and feasts. Families gather together before tables prepared with foods and candles. These Kwanzaa tables are set with the symbols of Kwanzaa:

- A straw mat, which stands for the foundation of the family
- A seven-candle candleholder, which stands for the family background
- Seven candles, which stand for the seven principles of life
- An ear of corn, which stands for the cycle of fruitfulness and having children
- A unity cup, which stands for togetherness
- A straw basket, which represents the harvest
- Crops, which are the fruit of hard work and harvest efforts
- Rewards, which are for good and hard work

The candles are lighted for the seven principles of unity, self-determination, collective work and responsibility, cooperative economics, purpose, creativity, and faith.

*[The remainder of this text can be used if desired to enhance the table top exhibit. These portions of text can be mounted on construction paper with tagboard triangles to stand upright on the table, or they can be made into posters and mounted on the wall.]*

From *Classroom Museums: Touchable Tables for Kids*, published by GoodYear Books. Copyright © 1992 Pamela Marx.

# Traditional Holiday Colors

## Christmas

*Red* is for charity. It is a bold color used in candy canes, ribbons, and ornaments.

*Green* is for the promise of spring. It is seen in the evergreens of the season, ivy, holly, mistletoe, and the Christmas tree.

*White* is for purity. It is seen in stars, lights, angels, and snowflake decorations.

*Gold* is for sunlight. It is seen in tinsel, garlands, stars, and ornaments.

## Hanukkah

*Blue* and *white* are the colors of the Israeli flag.

*Yellow* is also commonly seen and may signify the candlelight of the menorah.

## Chinese New Year

*Red* is for good luck.

# Special Holiday Foods

## Christmas

**Mexico**—Tamales

**Germany**—Pfeffernuesse cookies, marzipan (sweet almond paste)

**England**—Mince pies, plum puddings, fruitcake

**Scandinavia**—Rice pudding with a hidden lucky almond

**Chile**—Hot meat pies

**Holland**—Gingerbread cookies

**America**—Pumpkin pies, roast turkey and stuffing

**Italy**—Pannetone (sponge cake with currants/ raisins)

**Greece**—Christpomo (nut cakes)

**Switzerland**—Ringli (extra large doughnuts)

## Hanukkah

Latkes (potato pancakes)

## New Year

**Japan**—Soba noodles served with hot soup, mochi (pounded rice cakes)

**Korea**—Ttukgook (rice soup)

**Scotland**—Spiced ale

**China**—Candied melon, candied coconut, watermelon seeds

## Harvest Festivals

**India**—Pongal (sweet made of rice, sugar, fruit, and butter oil)

**African-American**—Black-eyed peas, sweet potato pie

From *Classroom Museums: Touchable Tables for Kids*, published by GoodYear Books. Copyright © 1992 Pamela Marx.

**Teacher Resources**

## Discussion Guidelines

*If you discuss this table using the following guidelines, your presentation will be easier if you are familiar with several of the legends, historical events, and stories that surround many winter holiday traditions. Some are included in the table text.*

*Does someone in your school observe a unique tradition such as Sweden's St. Lucia Day or the Polish Christmas celebration called Wigilia (vee-geel-ya)? Some of these traditions involve feast tables set up in particular ways or other displays that can be re-created on your discussion day. If you are fortunate enough to have such a person, ask him or her to make a presentation on the particular customs with which he or she is familiar. Children find these stories fascinating. Caution any such speakers to avoid religious references as much as possible.*

## General

What happens here in winter that is different from other times of the year?

> *Cold*        *Days are short*

Did you know that the winter has always been a time when people have had celebrations? What kinds of things do you celebrate in winter—especially in December?

> *Christmas      Hanukkah      New Year*
> *Thanksgiving and other harvest festivals*

Why do you think people have celebrations?

> *They are happy.*
> *Something special has happened.*
> *They want to remember something important.*
> *Celebrations are fun.*

Ancient people celebrated in the middle of winter because this was the time of the solstice, the shortest day of the year. The sun's ways seemed mysterious. When the days began to grow longer again, people were happy and wanted to celebrate the victory of the sun over the cold and frost.

Think of all the different winter holidays you named. Let's talk about some of them.

> *[Detailed descriptions of the holidays are not provided here but can be gleaned directly from the table text, which is short and straightforward. Let the table text and your touchables help you decide what to discuss about the exhibit.]*

## Christmas

The origins of the Christmas tree

Ornament origins

St. Nicholas Day in Holland

St. Lucia Day in Sweden

Las Posadas in Mexico

Traditional foods and sweets from different countries

Holiday greenery—poinsettias, mistletoe, holly

Advent traditions such as wreath and calendar

## Hanukkah

The story of Judah and the Maccabees

How the menorah is used

The game of dreidel and how it is played

The miracle of the oil

## New Year Celebrations

How do people prepare for the new year?

What is exciting about the idea of a whole new year?

How would you celebrate a new year?

How do other people celebrate it?

### China

The new year's celebration is called Sun Nin.

> Five-day festival
> Red is color of good luck.
> Gifts of money are wrapped in red and placed on money tree for children.
> Dragon Parade is a main event.
> Scrolls bearing goodwill messages decorate homes.

*From Classroom Museums: Touchable Tables for Kids,* published by GoodYear Books. Copyright © 1992 Pamela Marx.

## Japan

The new year's celebration is called Oshogatsu.

> Children fly kites.
> Decorations are rope, bamboo, and pine.
> Rope means hope for a sunny, bright new year.
> Bamboo means strength and vitality.
> Pine means stability and long life.
> Sun Goddess legend

## Vietnam

The new year's celebration is called Tet Festival.

> Paper money is made and burned to honor ancestors.
> First footers tradition
> Carp, a freshwater fish, is a symbol.

## Korea

The new year's celebration is called Solnal.

> Gifts of money and fruit are given.
> Ttukgook, special rice soup, is eaten.

## India

Hindus celebrate four new years, one for each season.

> The autumn celebration, called Diwali, is most popular.
> Festival of Lights
> Clay dishes (dipas) hold lights and are placed every-where.
> Note similarity with Southwest luminaria tradition.

# Harvest Celebrations

## India

Pongal is rice harvest festival in India.

> Occurs in January
> Rice is fed to cows.
> Cows are decorated.

## Iroquois

Mid-Winter Festival celebrates harvest.

> Occurs in January
> Feasting and ceremonial dances

## African-American

Kwanzaa celebrates harvest and family values.

> Kwanzaa symbols
> Seven principles of life

1. Have children try a new taste treat. They can easily make mincemeat turnovers the same way children in Victorian England did, with scraps of pie crust from the holiday pie.

## Mincemeat Pie

For a class of approximately thirty students, use a box of prepared crusts (two crusts to a box). Flour your working area lightly and press the two crusts out slightly to make them a little larger and more square in shape. Cut four-inch squares of dough. Fill each with one teaspoon of prepared mincemeat. Fold and press edges down with fork and sprinkle with sugar. Bake at temperature recommended on box until lightly brown.

If prepared mincemeat is too expensive, you can make your own by grating six large peeled apples and mixing the grated apples with one cup of raisins, four tablespoons of sugar, and one-quarter teaspoon of cinnamon.

2. You can make simple paper-bag piñatas for Las Posadas. Use lunch-size brown paper bags. Cut tissue paper strips approximately one and one-half inch wide. Tissue paper should be in bright colors. Students should fringe each strip to about three-quarter inch. Beginning at the bottom of the bag and moving up with the fringed end down, students glue fringe to bag in rows until the bag is covered with fringe. Drop a few pieces of candy in bag and staple closed. Add a yarn or string handle. Hang the piñata for decoration.

3. Prepared latke mixes are available in most grocery stores. These mixes are virtually foolproof and quite tasty. Have the students make potato pancakes for Hanukkah. Serve with applesauce.

4. Learn to play dreidel. A dreidel is a four-sided top with different markings on each side. The markings are called *nun, hey, gimmel,* and *shin.* Two to eight people play. Each player starts with five nuts or pennies. Everybody puts one of their pennies in the pot. Then the game starts. Players take turns spinning the dreidel. If it lands with nun up, the player gets nothing. If it lands with shin up, the player gives one penny to the pot. If it lands with gimmel up, the player takes all the pennies in the pot. If it lands on hey, the player takes half the pennies in the pot. When the pot runs out after a gimmel, each player puts one penny in the pot and the game resumes. The winner is the player with the most pennies at the end of play.

From *Classroom Museums: Touchable Tables for Kids,* published by GoodYear Books. Copyright © 1992 Pamela Marx.

5. Make a window dragon for Chinese New Year. Before they begin, have children peruse stories and materials containing pictures of Chinese new year dragons. Then, lay out waxed paper. Have children trace or sketch the shape of a dragon head with pencils. Their traced shapes can be as simple as circles or squares. Make them nine to twelve inches in diameter. With solution of one part white glue and one part water, children paint with the liquid and affix red and yellow tissue squares. Then, using picture books as visual resources, have them glue on eyes and mouths cut out of construction paper. When dry, trim excess waxed paper. Punch holes at top to insert yarns for hanging. Children can decorate their dragons with feathers and other ornamentations if they wish.

6. For Japanese New Year, have children make a pine tree using the art of paper cutting (kirigami). At Oshogatsu, the pine tree is cut and placed by the front door for luck. To make a kirigami tree, children start with a rectangle (one by two inches) of brown construction paper and a triangle (four by six by six inches) of green. Cut V-shaped notches from the sides and top of the triangle. Save the cutout shapes. Then, glue the brown trunk to an 8 $\frac{1}{2}$-by-11-inch sheet of paper. Lay out the notched triangle above the trunk and place the cutouts in the notches allowing about one-quarter inch of paper to show between the notched triangle and the cutouts. Glue the triangle and the cutouts down above the trunk.

7. The Iroquois made corn-husk masks for some ceremonies. Have students work with corn husks. Soak husks for one hour in water. Give older children two large husks. Have them split the husks into one-half inch strips. Make ten to twelve slits in one side of a shoe-box lid about $\frac{1}{4}$ to $\frac{3}{8}$ inch apart. Insert ends of split husks in these spaces. Using an over/under weave, have children weave remaining husks into small mats. Paint weaving with solution of one part white glue and one part water. When dry, remove completed weaving from box top and glue to sheet of paper. This activity gives children an idea of how difficult it is to work with cornhusks to make masks and other items. (Note: A straw mat is a symbol for Kwanzaa. Corn is also a Kwanzaa symbol. This small mat could be woven as an example of the Kwanzaa symbol that stands for the foundation of the family.) Younger children can make cornhusk masks. Cut two eye holes out of paper plates and tape on popsicle stick handles. Cut cornhusks into small pieces. Have children glue them onto the paper plates, covering the plates entirely.

8. Make an easier version of the Advent calendar activity sheet. Have children cut out trees and glue twenty-four hard candies to them as "decorations." Then, they can enjoy eating one candy a day until Christmas.

From *Classroom Museums: Touchable Tables for Kids*, published by GoodYear Books. Copyright © 1992 Pamela Marx.

From *Classroom Museums: Touchable Tables for Kids*, published by GoodYear Books. Copyright © 1992 Pamela Marx.

## Resources

1.  Refer to the Discussion Guidelines for this chapter. Several suggestions are given there for possible speakers for a winter festival table. In addition, local community cultural clubs and churches may have members who will share special customs of their ancestral countries. Parents in your school may know someone from these community groups who will speak to students.

    Children love to hear folktales, so you might focus the discussion on holiday folklore. Perhaps the librarian from the school or community library will speak. Several Caldecott winning books deal with Christmas traditions, and some beautifully illustrated recent books tell interesting and delightful stories about Hanukkah. A selection of these books is included at the end of this section.

    You might also try to find a college student to speak on your exhibit. A student of comparative cultures would be a good choice. Check with your local college.

2.  There are many good books available to read in conjunction with this table. Some provide good craft and activity ideas.

    *Baboushka and the Three Kings* by Ruth Robbins, published by Parnassus Press (1960) (Caldecott Medal winner).

    *Nine Days to Christmas, A Story of Mexico* by Marie Hall Ets and Aurora Labastida, published by Viking Press (1959) (Caldecott Medal winner).

    *Hershel and the Hanukkah Goblins* by Eric Kimmel, published by Holiday House (1989).

    *The Polar Express* by Chris Van Allsburg, published by Houghton Mifflin Company (1985) (Caldecott Medal winner).

    *A Child's Christmas in Wales* by Dylan Thomas, published by David R. Godine (1980).

    *The Chinese New Year* by Cheng Hou-tien, published by Holt, Rinehart and Winston (1976).

    *Happy New Year Round the World* by Lois Johnson, published by Rand McNally and Company (1966).

    *Lion Dancer* by Kate Waters and Madeline Slovenz-Low, published by Scholastic (1990).

    *Gung Hay Fat Choy* by June Behrens, published by Childrens Press (1982).

    *The Kwanza Coloring Book* by Valerie J. R. Banks, published by Sala Enterprises (1985).

    *Kwanzaa* by Deborah M. Newton Chocolate, published by Children's Press (1990).

    *Hanukkah* by Miriam Chaikin, published by Holiday House (1990).

    *Hanukkah* by Malka Drucker, published by Holiday House (1980) (craft, recipe, and game resource book).

    *Matsuri: Festival* by Nancy Araki and Jane Horii, published by Heian International Publishing Company (1978).

Name_____ Date _____

## Make your own Advent Calendar.

**Advent calendars were first used in Germany.** You can make your own. Color in the pictures on the Christmas tree. Number the circles below 1 through 24. Cut out the circles and place them randomly on the pictures on the tree. Place a tiny dot of glue on the tab at the top of each numbered circle. Glue the tab part of each circle to the tree. As each day in December passes, pull off the circle for that day to reveal the picture behind it.

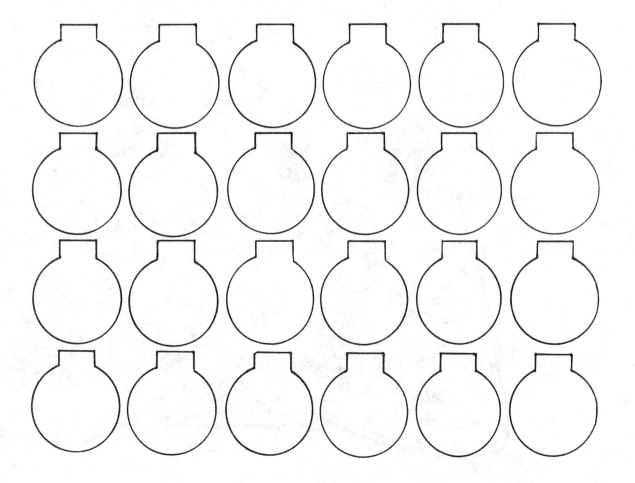

From *Classroom Museums: Touchable Tables for Kids*, published by GoodYear Books. Copyright © 1992 Pamela Marx.

From *Classroom Museums: Touchable Tables for Kids*, published by GoodYear Books. Copyright © 1992 Pamela Marx.

Winter Festivals Around the World

Name_____ Date _____

**Can you match the winter celebration with its country?**

| | |
|---|---|
| 1. Diwali | Sweden |
| 2. Kwanzaa | India |
| 3. Oshogatsu | Vietnam |
| 4. Las Posadas | Japan |
| 5. Hogmanay | Holland |
| 6. St. Lucia Day | Mexico |
| 7. Sun Nin | African-American |
| 8. St. Nicholas Day | Scotland |
| 9. Tet | China |

**Circle the holidays that celebrate the new year.**

**In how many languages can you say Merry Christmas? Match the greeting with its country.**

| | |
|---|---|
| 1. Feliz Navidad | Italy |
| 2. Joyeux Noel | Germany |
| 3. Merry Christmas | United States |
| 4. Buon Natale | Holland |
| 5. Vrolijk Kerstfeest | France |
| 6. Fröliche Weihnachten | Mexico |

From *Classroom Museums: Touchable Tables for Kids*, published by GoodYear Books. Copyright © 1992 Pamela Marx.

# Fibers and Fabrics

*The purpose of this exhibit is to help children look at everyday items, in this case cloth or rope, in a new way. Nearly everything we use and do has a rich and interesting history. This subject is a window on thousands of years of people learning to make use of the natural resources around them. It also offers an opportunity to think about how technological advances have changed our daily lives.*

From *Classroom Museums: Touchable Tables for Kids*, published by GoodYear Books. Copyright © 1992 Pamela Marx.

## Teacher Guidance

### Getting Started

Read the table text to familiarize yourself with basic information about wool, cotton, and silk and to get ideas about other fibers you might want to use as touchables—polyester, rayon, coir (coconut), sisal, and jute.

Because a demonstration of spinning or weaving is so valuable in conjunction with this exhibit, make the identification of such a craftsperson an early priority. Using the suggestions in the Resource section of this chapter, ask a parent to start exploring the availability of such people.

### Curriculum Integration

This exhibit can be integrated into your classroom curriculum in several ways.

1. **Literature:** Some school districts have identified *A New Coat for Anna* as a possible core literature selection for second- and third-graders. If yours is one, this table and the suggested student activities complement the story elements directly and offer an easy way to incorporate reading themes into both science and social studies.

2. **Life Sciences:** A silkworm display offers a perfect opportunity to integrate insect or butterfly life-cycle studies into exhibit preparation. For lower grades, introduce sheep as a fiber source with your regular farm animal studies. For all grades, the discussion of fibrous plants—grasses, cotton, and others—allows this table to mesh thematically with studies on plants and how they grow.

3. **World Geography:** People grow plants and raise animals around the world to supply fiber for clothing and fabric. Make this a part of your discussions of world geography.

4. **Social Studies:** This exhibit dovetails with discussions on technology and the development of industrialization. The exhibit is an excellent jumping off point for analysis of how technology changes lives.

5. **History:** History studies, whether world, national, or state, involve analysis of periods of history when spinning wheels and carding tools were part of daily life. This exhibit, especially if presented in conjunction with a spinning demonstration, can bring to life a part of history that we usually see only in movies or described in books.

6. **Physical Sciences:** Use different types of fabric swatches to create static electricity. Have swatches of flannel (synthetic and cotton), wool, and polyester available together with a plastic spoon and a Ping-Pong ball. Rub the convex side of the spoon rapidly over the cloth. Does it gather static electricity? Put it next to a student's hair. Does the hair stand up? Once the spoon has gathered static electricity, try to drag the Ping-Pong ball across the table using the electricity in the spoon. Do different fabrics work better than others?

# Table Appearance

*As with all the exhibit tables, copy the table text and place it in front of the exhibit touchables for easy readability. The text enhances the value of the touchables for older students and gives adults an easy reference when explaining the table to younger children.*

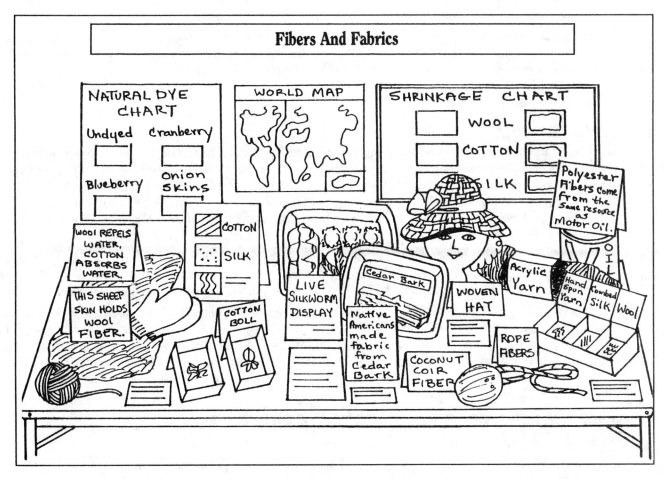

Make sure you identify all of your samples. If you get fibers in different processing stages (raw, dirty, cleaned, and uncombed and combed), mark this information on the container holding them.

Group your fiber samples by type on the table. The three primary areas of your exhibit will probably be wool, cotton, and silk. A last section of the table can be devoted to synthetics and basket and rope fibers. Any section of the table can include samples of hand-dyed fabric or yarn.

To display swatches of fabric, glue them to small pieces of posterboard (about three inches square) and label them. Glue only one side of the swatch down so the fabric can be touched and its texture felt. Use small paper plates or old microwave dishes to display yarns, seeds, and unprocessed fibers. You might staple part of the yarn or other touchable to the plate so that it remains with its label.

Try the following exhibit organization:

**Flax Section:** If you have linen cloth or flax, use this near the first part of the table in conjunction with the introductory text.

**Cotton Section:** With a little advanced planning, this section of the exhibit can be more interesting than you might think. Certainly, cotton cloth, yarn, and balls will give the children the feel and look of cotton fiber. Depending upon the part of the country in which you live, local agricultural fairs can be a good source of cotton seeds and ginned cotton seeds. These are useful additions to the table. Also, include examples of the cotton boll itself or pictures of the growing plant. Have polyester fiberfill on hand so that children can compare the difference between cotton fiber and polyester fiber. Place small samples like seeds in small containers with labels.

From *Classroom Museums: Touchable Tables for Kids*, published by GoodYear Books. Copyright © 1992 Pamela Marx.

**Wool Section:** A sheep's skin rug, wool yarn, wool cloth, wool mittens or clothing, alpaca jacket, and any other woolen articles can be used here. Mark your touchables with tags or adhesive labels. Make sure to have some acrylic articles on hand so the children can feel the difference between wool (a natural fiber) and acrylic (a human-made fiber).

**Silk Section:** This part of the table is especially fun if you have a live silkworm exhibit. If you have no silkworm eggs, check with your local preschools. Preschool teachers often keep refrigerated eggs for use from year to year. Perhaps they can share a few with you. In addition to the silkworms, this part of the table can include silk swatches, samples of silk-like polyester (for comparison), and pictures of silkworms and silkworm farms.

**Other Fibers Section:** This section of the exhibit has two parts. In a display of human-made fibers, include examples of the materials from which those fibers are made (coal, limestone, and ginned cotton seed fuzz, for example), as well as samples of the fibers and fabrics themselves. The second part of this section should include fibers used for ropes, mats, and tropical cloths, such as coconut, sisal, raffia, jute, and hemp. Some Native Americans used cedar and other barks to make fabric. Display pieces of such barks.

## Sample Touchables

Possible touchables include swatches of cloth including muslins, burlap, linen, wool, 100 percent cotton, blends, polyester and silk; living silkworm display; cotton seeds, ginned cotton seeds, cotton bolls, cotton balls; sheep's skin rug, alpaca cloth; coconut; sisal, hemp, and other rope samples; bark, coal, wool, cotton, and silk yarn samples; white or natural yarn dyed with natural dyes such as cranberries, blueberries, brown onion skins. Be creative with the synthetic part of the exhibit. Ginned cotton seeds, coal, and oil are all processed to make fabric. With a can of motor oil, make the point that the same raw material in car oil can be processed to make beautiful polyester fabrics.

The timing of your table is important if you plan on a living silkworm exhibit. Silkworms need two things—mulberry leaves and time. Once mulberry leaves sprout, you can hatch eggs in seven to ten days. About three weeks after hatching, the worms are a good size for easy viewing. Consider these timing issues when planning this display.

Other touchables that add to the table but may be harder to come by are spinning wheels, carding tools, looms, and pictures of people spinning. While these may be less available than other touchables, you may be pleasantly surprised by things people have at home. Some people have decorative early American spinning wheel reproductions. Many people have looms of one sort or another at home; you could even use a child's play loom. Make sure you post a world map on the wall to help children visualize the history and current uses of fiber. The table text discusses many different geographic locations.

## Student Involvement in Table Preparation

Enlist student help in preparing the exhibit in several ways.

1.   Students can help prepare this exhibit by bringing fabric swatches, yarn, rope, and cord from home. Have children identify the types of fiber before they bring their samples to school. Children might also have articles of clothing made from unusual fibers to share with the exhibit.

2.   Have children make shrinkage and natural dye charts. For the shrinkage chart, use three five-inch-square swatches each of silk, cotton, wool, and polyester. Display the swatches on posterboard before contact with water, after contact with water and air dry, and after contact with water and heat dry in a dryer. Place any swatches that you dry in a dryer in a hosiery bag so they don't get lost. This chart will show shrinkage and wrinkling.

     For the natural dyes chart, begin with three-inch swatches of an unbleached muslin or white cotton fabric. Pick as many plant items as you can to dye the swatches, such as cranberries, blueberries, beets, brown onion skins, coffee, and tea. Dye a few swatches with modern dyes for contrast. Liquid dyes are easy to use. Mount the dyed swatches on posterboard, each with identification as to dye used and a sample swatch of undyed fabric for reference.

3.   Children can also participate directly in the layout and organization of touchables upon the table. They can follow the guidelines in the Table Appearance section of this chapter.

From *Classroom Museums: Touchable Tables for Kids*, published by GoodYear Books. Copyright © 1992 Pamela Marx.

*The table text concentrates on linen, wool, cotton and silk fibers. Feel free to add fibers to your exhibit which are not discussed in the text. Identify them with tags. Perhaps students can do research on fibers not discussed at length here.*

**Uses**

## Fibers and Fabrics

*What is fiber? Fiber is material from which rope, cloth, and baskets can be made. Short threads of fiber are twisted into longer strands. These long strands are used to make strong rope and cloth.*

*In this exhibit, we will explore the different kinds of fiber. We will focus on those natural fibers used to make most of the cloth we use and wear everyday. These fibers are cotton, wool, and silk. We will also look at some human-made fibers and fibers that are used primarily for making baskets, ropes, and mats.*

## Learning to Use Fiber

*Early people probably made their clothes from whole animal skins. But as time passed and tools developed, people learned how to use plants that grew around them and the fur of certain animals that lived near them to make yarns, fabrics, cord, and rope. Flax plants gave people fiber for lightweight linen fabric. Silkworms gave people fiber for beautiful silks. Agave plants gave people sisal fiber for strong rope and cord. Sheep and llamas gave people fiber for warm water-repellant wool clothing. Cotton plants gave people fiber for absorbent cotton fabric. Over time, people learned how to use fibers to help them in their work and to make their homes and clothing more comfortable.*

*Today, as throughout history, flax is soaked, sheep are sheared, cotton is picked, silkworm cocoons are boiled, but then what happens? To be useful, these fibers must be spun into yarns and threads. How have these processes changed over the years?*

## Cleaning and Straightening

After the fibers are collected from plant or animal, they must be cleaned and combed. First they are washed to remove dirt and dust, and then they are straightened. In the past, people combed fibers by hand with *carding boards* to straighten them. Today this process is done by machine. Once fiber is combed, it is ready for spinning.

## Spinning

*Spinning* is the process of twisting short fibers into long threads. Before the invention of the spinning wheel, people spun yarn by hand with a *spindle* and a *distaff*. The distaff was a pole that held bunches of combed fibers. The spinner pulled fibers from the distaff. As she did this, she twisted them in one direction and hooked them onto the spindle. The spindle was a spool at the spinner's side on which she wound the spun yarn. It hung down from her other hand.

From *Classroom Museums: Touchable Tables for Kids*, published by GoodYear Books. Copyright © 1992 Pamela Marx.

After twisting the fiber onto the spindle, the spinner might set the spindle spinning opposite the way she had spun the fiber off the distaff. This tight double twist made the thread or yarn strong. When the spindle fell to the floor, the spinner stopped. She wound more yarn onto the spindle and began again.

The spinning wheel made spinning yarn much easier. It was invented in India. A big wheel was attached by a belt to the spindle. This made spinning much faster. Today we use huge machines to spin thread and yarn.

Can you imagine having to spin each yarn or thread of the clothes you wear? After you spin the yarn, you weave the cloth. After you weave the cloth, you sew the clothes. You probably would not have as many clothes.

## Weaving

Once thread or yarn is spun, it must be woven into fabric. *Weaving* is a way of turning threads into a large, flat sheet of cloth, matting, or carpeting.

Weaving is done on a *loom*. *Warp* threads are strung onto a loom in one direction. Then, the weaver takes other threads and crosses them over and under these warp threads. These cross threads are called the *weft* or *woof*. The weft threads are rolled onto a stick to take them back and forth across the warp. The stick is called the *shuttle*.

At one time, all weaving was done on hand looms. Eventually, advances in technology made weaving easier and faster. First came foot pedals. The pedals raised certain warp threads so the shuttle went back and forth faster. Then came the flying shuttle. It made weaving even faster. Today, huge power looms weave threads very quickly into cloth.

Weavers use many different styles. They create styles and designs by changing the number and pattern of the warp threads they cross with the weft.

Two different styles of weave are the linen weave and the canvas weave.

## Some of the Many Different Fibers We Use Today

### Flax: A Soft Fiber Made from a Plant

Flax was probably the first fiber people used. The Egyptians grew flax at least 7,000 years ago. Flax is a *bast* fiber. Bast fibers are soft fibers taken from the stems of woody, fibrous plants. The soft inner fiber is used to make linen thread.

Leading flax producers today are Canada, Argentina, India, Russia, and the United States. In the United States, most flax is grown in North and South Dakota.

How is flax prepared to make cloth or rope?

Farmers harvest the stems of the flax plant before the seeds ripen. They tie these stems in bundles and soak them. This is called *retting*. Retting causes the stems to rot. This makes it easier to remove the fibers from the plant. Once retting is finished, the stems dry in the sun or ovens.

Next, workers break and *scutch* the dried stems. Scutching is the process of removing the fiber from the wood, leaves, and broken pieces of the flax plant. Rope is made from the broken pieces of flax.

The longer flax fibers are combed to prepare them for spinning threads to weave fabric. The combed flax is light yellow. Its fibers are eight to twenty inches in length. Flax is one of the strongest natural fibers.

Other bast fibers are hemp, ramie, and jute. Jute is not a strong fiber, but it is cheap. A course cloth called *burlap* is often made from jute. Burlap is sometimes used to make bags to store grain and produce.

From *Classroom Museums: Touchable Tables for Kids*, published by GoodYear Books. Copyright © 1992 Pamela Marx.

Fibers and Fabrics

## Cotton: The Mystery Fiber

Historians do not know how people began to use cotton as a fiber. They do know that about 4,000 years ago, people in Peru grew it, spun it, and made cloth. Ancient mummy wrappings from Peru prove this. Meanwhile, on the other side of the world in India, people also grew, spun, and wove cotton. It was not used in Egypt or Europe until about 2,500 years ago.

Today, cotton is probably the most widely used fiber in the world. It washes easily and absorbs water well. Cotton grows in warm parts of the world in many different countries such as Egypt, Brazil, India, Russia, China, the United States, Mexico, and Argentina.

Cotton fiber comes from the seedpod of the cotton plant. This pod is called the *boll.* Most growing cotton is white, but there are also pink, yellow, and red varieties. Cotton blossoms last only about a day and then the seed boll starts to form. The boll has five different compartments with about nine seeds in each of them. A thick mass of soft material surrounds the seeds. This soft material is the cotton fiber. It is picked out of the boll.

Picked cotton is then *ginned.* In the ginning process, a machine removes the seeds from the soft material. Workers pack the soft cotton into bales and send it to factories for cleaning, combing, and spinning. While these processes were once done by hand, now huge automated machines do the work.

## Wool: An Animal Fiber

Wool is the furry covering that grows on some mammals. Most wool comes from sheep, but some comes from other animals like goats, llamas, and camels. Animals from which we get wool are raised around the world in many countries including Australia, Russia, China, Argentina, South Africa, Turkey, Great Britain and the United States.

Although wool grows on the skin of animals, it is different from hair because the outside of wool is made up of tiny scales. The fibers are also very curly. The scales and curls of wool fibers make them stick together when they are spun into yarn.

Wool can do something else that other fiber cannot do as easily. It can *felt.* This means that you can press the fibers together tightly to make felt fabric without spinning and weaving.

To get wool from sheep, it is cut, or *sheared,* off the animal. This is done once or twice a year. Workers sort the cut wool into long and short fibers. They pack it into bales and send it to the mill for further processing. At the mill, wool is cleaned, carded, and spun into yarn or thread.

Wool has many unique characteristics. Natural oils in wool repel water. This makes wool especially good for snow and cold weather clothing. Wool shrinks when wet and dried. Moths will damage wool. They lay their eggs in the fiber. When the eggs hatch, larvae eat the keratin (protein) and grease they find around the wool fibers. As they search for these nutrients, they eat holes in the wool fabric.

From *Classroom Museums: Touchable Tables for Kids,* published by GoodYear Books. Copyright © 1992 Pamela Marx.

## Silk: Fiber from a Worm

All natural fibers except one are short and must be spun to make a long thread. The exception is silk. Silk threads are naturally long and unbroken. These very thin threads make silkworm cocoons. To make silk, the cocoon is unwound.

Silk making began in China nearly 4,000 years ago. The Chinese kept the process secret for almost 2,500 years. This made silk a very rare and expensive fabric. Traders and explorers carried it from China thousands of miles to customers in Europe.

Today, the Far East (China, Japan, South Korea, and Thailand) produces much silk, but it also comes from other countries such as Brazil, India, and Russia.

Silk is made by silkworms. A silkworm is the caterpillar stage of a white moth. They are raised for their silk on special farms. When the moth eggs hatch into caterpillars, workers place them on trays and feed them mulberry tree leaves. The newly hatched caterpillars are black. They are so small that they almost look like tiny bits of dirt. Their job is to eat and grow. They grow fast into grayish worms that shed their skins. After five or six weeks of eating and growing, silkworms spin cocoons. From these cocoons, silk threads are unravelled.

Before the moths emerge from their cocoons, the cocoons are dropped in boiling water. This kills the moths and also loosens the silk fibers. The silk fibers are then rolled onto reels. Several fibers are twisted together at one time to make silk thread because one fiber alone is not strong enough. These reeled threads are called *raw* silk.

Sometimes silk fiber is harvested from cocoons from which the moths have hatched so that they can lay new eggs. Since these cocoons have holes in them, their threads cannot be unwoven in single strands. The broken cocoons are combed and spun into *spun* silk.

## Other Natural Fibers

*Other fibers from plants are used in different parts of the world. Some are used to make rope and baskets. Some are used to make cloth.*

### Other Natural Fibers **Sisal**

This is a thick, stiff fiber. It comes from the leaves of the agave plant. Eastern Africa is the world's leading sisal producer. People make rope and cord from agave. Sometimes they weave the rope into mats or braid it into rugs.

### Other Natural Fibers **Coir (koy-uhr)**

This fiber is made from the hairy outside covering of coconuts. People could make it into cloth or twist it into rope. Coir rope rots in fresh water but becomes even stronger in salt water. As a result, people use coir ropes on oceangoing boats.

### Other Natural Fibers **Raffia**

People use the leaves of an African palm tree to make this fiber. They make baskets and straw hats with it.

From *Classroom Museums: Touchable Tables for Kids*, published by GoodYear Books. Copyright © 1992 Pamela Marx.

Fibers and Fabrics

### Other Natural Fibers **Hemp**

This strong fiber comes from a plant native to central and western Asia. It is used for making rope, twine, and other cording.

### Other Natural Fibers **Jute**

Jute is a rough fiber. Big jute producers are China, Bangladesh, and India. It is not a strong fiber, but it is inexpensive. Jute is often used to make burlap cloth. People use burlap to make bags or sacks for holding grains and other produce.

### Other Natural Fibers **Bark**

Some Native Americans processed barks of local trees such as cedar to make cloth.

## Human-made Fibers

There are other fibers, too. Many new fibers are made by humans. We use chemicals to turn things like limestone and natural gas, coal and oil, and the fuzz around ginned cotton seeds into fabrics. During this processing, threads are created chemically and spun into yarns and thread.

*Rayon* is the oldest human-made fiber. We use the cellulose from wood pulp and the fuzz from ginned cotton seeds to make it.

*Polyester* is a popular fiber made from coal and oil. Polyester fiber is useful because it resists shrinking and wrinkling.

*Acrylic* fiber is made from limestone and natural gas. Yarns and sweaters are often made from acrylic.

**Human-made**

From *Classroom Museums: Touchable Tables for Kids,* published by GoodYear Books. Copyright © 1992 Pamela Marx.

## Discussion Guidelines

*These discussion guidelines are designed to make two points. First, they help children see that some things we take for granted, such as cloth and rope, began as plants or animals in some distant or nearby corner of the world. Second, the technical development of spinning and weaving demonstrates how machinery and tools can transform life.*

What do you see on this table?

> *Cloth   Yarn   Rope*
> *Mat    Coconut  Cotton balls*
> *Sheepskin rug*

What do these things have in common?

Of what material are they made? What material is found on or in them?

> *Fiber*

Where are fibers found?

> *Animals  Plants  Cocoons*

To what uses do we put fibers?

> *Ropes, baskets, mats, and other useful items*
> *Clothing, hats, mittens, coats*
> *Rugs, mats, and decorative weavings and hangings*

From what animals do we get fibers?

> *Sheep, llamas, goats, camels*

What fibers come from these animals?

> *The curly, scaly fur is called wool.*

How do we get it from the animal?

> *It is sheared off.*

How is it processed after it is taken from the animal?

> *Cleaned  Spun*
> *Combed  Woven*

Why is wool used for some things and not others?

> *It contains natural oils that make it water resistant.*
> *It is curly and stretchy. When woven into cloth, it traps air to insulate the wearer.*

What are its special qualities?

> *It breathes.*
> *It is water resistant.*
> *It keeps you warm.*

What are some of its problems?

> *It shrinks in water.*
> *It is subject to invasion by moths.*

What other creature from the animal world gives us a fiber?

> *Silkworm*

How does the silkworm give us a fiber?

> *Silk comes from the strong threads the silkworm uses to weave its cocoon.*

Where was silk first taken from the silkworm and used to make cloth?

> *China*

How is silk taken from the cocoon?

> *Cocoons are boiled.*
> *The silk strands are unwound onto reels.*
> *Silk from broken cocoons is combed.*

How is it then processed?

> *Spun   Woven*

What are the special benefits of silk?

> *Lightweight fabric*
> *Strong  Very beautiful*

What are the limitations of silk?

> *It can shrink when wet.*

What plants give us fibers?

> *Cotton, flax, agave, coconut, jute, hemp, raffia palm.*

Which one is most important today?

> *Cotton*

How does cotton grow?

> *It grows on a plant. Soft cotton fiber is the material found around the seeds in the seed boll.*

What part of the plant is picked to make cotton?

> *The soft material and the seeds are picked from the boll.*

From *Classroom Museums: Touchable Tables for Kids*, published by GoodYear Books. Copyright © 1992 Pamela Marx.

How is this processed?

*Ginned (to remove seeds)*
*Baled*
*Washed*
*Combed*
*Spun*
*Woven*

What do we make from cotton?

*Clothes*          *Rugs*
*Sheets*           *Curtains*

What are cotton's special qualities?

*It absorbs water.*
*It breathes.*
*It is lightweight.*

Does it shrink?

*Yes.*

Some fibers come from tall grasses. Can you name one?

*Flax*

What makes these fibers more suitable for spinning and weaving than others? Are they stronger?

*Yes.*

Are the fibers that come from them longer and more usable?

*Yes.*

What fabric do we make from flax?

*Linen*

From what kinds of fiber is rope made?

*Many—hemp, sisal, cotton, coir, jute*

Think of all the sources from which we get fiber.

*Plants*          *Animals*

Are there any other sources?

What about human-made fibers?

*Polyester*     *Rayon*     *Acrylic*

What are some of these fibers made of?

*Ginned cotton seed fuzz (rayon)*
*Coal, air, water, and oil (polyester)*
*Limestone, natural gas, air, water, and oil (acrylic)*
*Wood pulp cellulose (rayon) (acetate)*

What are their special qualities?

*Water repellent*
*Low shrinkage*
*Non-wrinkling*

## Student Activities

1.  Make a fiber chart. This project is a more detailed version of the fiber chart in this chapter's activity sheets. Ask children to look for fibers around their homes. They can collect swatches of cloth, pieces of rope and string, cotton balls, coconuts, old woven placemats, baskets, and hats. They should look in their yards for any plants they think might yield good fibers. Bird of paradise leaves and other strong-leafed plants may yield some interesting long fibers.

    Have each child arrange his or her materials in a chart. The charts can be organized in several ways: 1. by origin, either plant, human made or animal; 2. by geography, from which part of the world did the fiber likely come; or 3. by use, such as for cloth, rope, mats, baskets, and so on.

2.  Before the advent of artificial dyes, bright color in fabric was a luxury. People made dyes from plants and rocks. Have children use natural dyes to dye white or unbleached cotton swatches. This exercise helps children to see one part of the historical process of making cloth and gives them an idea of how much labor was involved before machines freed us from so many tasks. It also shows how historically people relied on simple things available to them from nature. The easiest natural dyes come from brown onion skins (golden yellow), blueberries (purplish blue), and cranberries or beets (red). Give children swatches of an unbleached muslin cloth (perhaps three-by-six-inch rectangles) or an unbleached yarn. For yellow dye, have children remove the outer brown skins from six to ten large brown onions. Immerse in two cups of water in saucepan and heat to boiling. Simmer for ten minutes and cool. For blue and red dyes, use one cup of berries or beets in two cups of water. Heat to boiling, simmer for ten minutes, and cool. Once the dyes are cool, let children dip one half of their yarn or cloth into the dye of their choice. Wring out swatch and place on newspaper or paper towels to dry. Children can cut clothing shapes from their swatches and "dress" paper figures with them using glue.

From *Classroom Museums: Touchable Tables for Kids*, published by GoodYear Books. Copyright © 1992 Pamela Marx.

3. This is a project for older children. Give each child a cotton ball. Tell them that they must spin a piece of thread using only their hands. The child who makes a five-inch thread first wins. Remind the children how spinning is done. Thread is spun by twisting fibers. The fibers are twisted tightly as they are pulled from a mass of combed fibers. The winning fiber must be twisted sufficiently so that it does not break immediately when pulled. This project helps demonstrate to children how different our lives are today from those of our ancestors. Long ago people could not take cloth for granted.

4. Tie dye a shirt. This is not as big a mess as you might think if you do it outdoors on a nice day. Tell each child to wear old clothes and bring a t-shirt. Using liquid dyes in large plastic buckets, let children tie dye t-shirts. First, children tie together sections of their shirts—the sleeves, the chest, the hem—using string or rubber bands. Then, they dip parts of the shirts into the different dyes. Remind them to wring out shirts before moving to the next color. Dyes should be warm for best results. Leave shirts outside on asphalt, grass, or a fence to dry. Try to have one or two adults available to help.

## Resources

1. Spinning clubs and adult education centers are good sources of information about local spinning enthusiasts. Spinning is a fascinating hobby that has ardent followers all over. Many spinners dress in period clothing to present spinning demonstrations at craft and history fairs. They use many different kinds of yarn, some of which they dye themselves. They have their own wheels and carding tools. Such a hobbyist could put on an excellent demonstration in conjunction with your exhibit.

2. There are organizations in some cities dedicated to preservation of the arts and crafts of the past. The members of these organizations devote themselves to learning the traditional techniques of a craft such as spinning, weaving, or lacemaking. They often stage demonstrations at local museums. Try to find out about such organizations by contacting the education department of a museum near you. Perhaps a volunteer from one of these groups can demonstrate in conjunction with your exhibit.

3. Local arts collectives might be able to direct you to someone with special weaving skills who could bring a small loom to your school and do a weaving demonstration.

4. The local library is always a good source of books containing drawings and photographs of both historical and modern spinning and weaving practices. A number of nonfiction books are available on fibers:

*Fibers* by Irving and Ruth Adler, published by the John Day Company (1964).

*The First Book of Wool* by Betty Cavanna and George Russell Harrison, published by Franklin Watts (1966).

*Picking and Weaving* by Bijou Le Tord, published by Four Winds Press (1980). (This is a picture book for younger children.)

*Silkworms* by Sylvia Johnson, published by Lerner Publications Company (1982).

There are some very good fiction picture books to read in conjunction with this exhibit:

*A New Coat for Anna* by Harriet Ziefert, published by Alfred A. Knopf (1986).

*The Goat in the Rug* by Geraldine, as told to Charles L. Blood and Martin Link, published by Aladdin Books (1990).

*Charlie Needs a Cloak* by Tomie de Paola, published by Scholastic (1973).

From *Classroom Museums: Touchable Tables for Kids*, published by GoodYear Books. Copyright © 1992 Pamela Marx.

Fibers and Fabrics

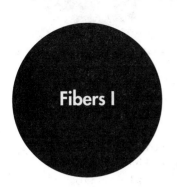

Fibers I

Name_____ Date _____

How Is Yarn Woven? Is it always woven the same way?

Color this area brown.

Color this area green.

Linen Weave
1 on 1

Canvas Weave
2 on 2

**After you have colored these two areas, cut them apart on the solid lines. Weave the strips together. Try the canvas or linen weave.**

From *Classroom Museums: Touchable Tables for Kids*, published by GoodYear Books. Copyright © 1992 Pamela Marx.

Name_____ Date _____

## My Fiber Chart

|  |  |
|---|---|
| Wool | Cotton |
| Silk | Synthetic |

Do these fibers feel different from one another?
How do they feel different?
How do they look different from one another?

From *Classroom Museums: Touchable Tables for Kids*, published by GoodYear Books. Copyright © 1992 Pamela Marx.

# Native Americans in Touch with the Land

*This exhibit illustrates Native Americans' respect for the lands on which they lived. At the same time, it provides a starting point for studies of local plants and animals and Native American ways of life.*

## Teacher Guidance

### Getting Started

To prepare for this table exhibit, read the table text to get a general idea of the differences among Native American ways of life in the United States. The text will also help you begin to think about what kind of display to do. You can either create models to represent different native North American ways of life, or you can focus on plants and animals in your area and how Native Americans used them.

While this chapter was designed to encourage an investigation of Native American traditions in your geographic region, you might decide to create an exhibit of model Native American villages representative of each part of the United States. Even if you go this route, make sure to couple the models with the touchables suggested in the Sample Touchables section of this chapter. The real value of this exhibit is in helping children think about bones, feathers, chunks of wood, and other natural objects the way Native Americans did. To the early peoples these things were tools, musical instruments, and decoration.

After looking over the table text, ask students to visit the library to check out a selection of books on different Native American ways of life around the country. Such books will contain photos and drawings helpful in making accurate model villages.

To do a local Native American exhibit, peruse the table text for your area of the country. Remember, it will give you only very general ideas about touchables. Then read the sample text on California Native Americans. This text gives you an example of how to proceed to create an exhibit on local ways of life. It is a simple, straightforward text that shows examples of regional plant and animal use.

Your next step will be to contact a local expert on wildlife, plants, or Native American lifeways. Locate nature centers, National Park Service ranger stations, and state preserves near you. These nature and wildlife centers employ rangers and train docents who are familiar with local flora and fauna. Someone should be able to advise you over the telephone about plants and animals that were important to local Native Americans. If you can visit the park site, ask a guide to point out local plants to use in your exhibit. Many of these plants probably still grow around your area in vacant lots and on undeveloped hillsides.

Check with natural history and Native American museums for information about native use of local plant and animal resources. Again, trained docents are very knowledgeable.

Reservations or local tribal councils have active memberships in many areas. These groups can be valuable sources of information and speakers, even in major metropolitan areas. Contact your city hall representatives for direction in reaching these groups. Powwows and other tribal events may be held routinely at local parks.

### Curriculum Integration

Integrate this exhibit project into your curriculum in several ways.

1. **American/Local History:** To achieve greater understanding of the Native American experience and perspective should be an integral goal of any study of American history. On the local level, too, a study of Native American life is an important part of any community history.

From *Classroom Museums: Touchable Tables for Kids*, published by GoodYear Books. Copyright © 1992 Pamela Marx.

2. **Life Sciences:** The investigation of local plant and animal life in an effort to understand Native American ways of life opens up the opportunity to discuss these natural elements on their own terms.

3. **Geography:** Study of Native American life leads into discussion of United States and regional geography. The places where early peoples lived are now parts of the United States.

4. **Earth Sciences:** Discussions about native life can lead to analysis of different habitat zones, geologic formations, and climates. Ask the docents with whom you speak how local climate and geologic formations directly affected Native American ways of life.

5. **Ecology:** Much can be learned from Native Americans' respect for the land upon which they live. Gathering what they needed to eat and killing only the animals that were necessary for survival, they wasted very little. Relate these things to environmental awareness studies.

6. **Art:** You can approach art in several ways. Introduce nineteenth-century artists who chose the frontier west as their subject, such as Frederick Remington and George Catlin. Choose an artist identified with a region, such as Georgia O'Keefe. (Study her work in relation to the Southwest where many different tribes live.) Locate examples of the work of a Native American artist, such as Harry Fonseca whose images of coyotes and other creatures are colorful and fascinating. Or, focus on traditional Native American art forms such as pottery, sand painting, and weaving.

## *Table Appearance*

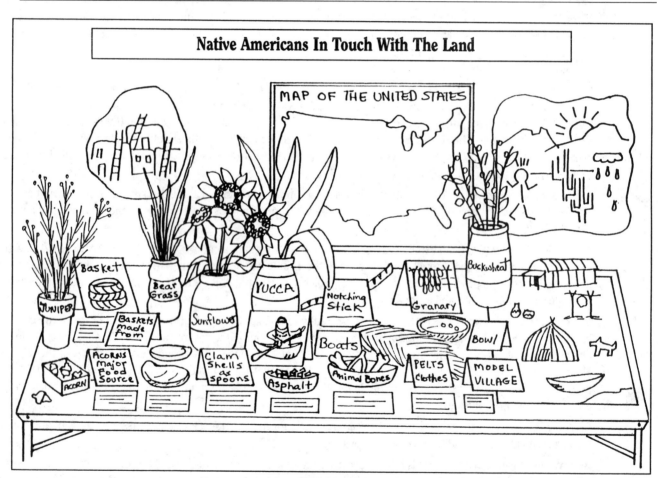

If you decide to do a model exhibit on Native Americans of North America, you will probably need two picnic-sized tables. Cover them with sponged newsprint. (See suggestions in Student Involvement section later in this chapter.) Plan to mount your models on pieces of plywood or double sheets of corrugated cardboard approximately thirty inches square. Place models on the table with the relevant table text nearby. Arrange your touchables between the models with labels to indicate their significance.

From *Classroom Museums: Touchable Tables for Kids*, published by GoodYear Books. Copyright © 1992 Pamela Marx.

If you do a table exhibit of local Native American life, you might include a model on the table. Group plant samples on one part of the table and animal remnants in another part. Try to locate pictures or drawings of animals in the context of local Native American life. Mount them on construction paper backed with tagboard triangles. Place them around the exhibit near relevant touchables.

Attractive and educational wall posters will enhance the exhibit. Display a wall-sized map of the United States so teachers can make connections with geography studies. Use the student pictograph described in the Student Involvement section as another wall exhibit.

## Sample Touchables

Let these suggestions for models start you thinking about possible touchables for a table on native North Americans in general.

**Grass Huts (West):** Create dome-shaped forms upon which dried grass can be glued. This can be done by layering papier-mâché over crumpled newspaper, or by cutting Styrofoam balls or eggs in half.

**Longhouses (Northeast):** Paint a shoe box brown and cover it with bark to simulate the look of a northeastern longhouse.

**Tepees (Plains):** Use wooden barbecue skewers or shish kebab sticks to create the conical shape of a tepee. Cover with a piece of unbleached muslin. Prior to attaching the muslin to the sticks, have students mark it with Native American designs.

**Pueblos (Southwest):** Use sugar cubes, gingerbread, or clay to create flat-topped pueblos.

**Plank houses (Northwest):** Construct plank houses with children's play logs.

Complete each model with cooking fires, granaries, trees, and small animals.

Between the models, place generic touchables with labels indicating possible use.

Sample touchables include cleaned chicken or beef bones, pelts, feathers, shells, wood/logs, fibrous local plants suitable for weaving baskets and mats, cattails, mosses, bark shavings, tar or pitch, and mortars and pestles.

If you choose to focus your exhibit on local Native American cultures, make your primary touchables a collection of local plants that Native Americans used. Find plants that performed a variety of functions as food, clothing, baskets, soap, deodorant, shelter, and medicine. Depending upon your location, appropriate touchables also include shells that people used for utensils and bowls, bark that they made into clothing, wood branches and twigs that they used for notching sticks and farm utensils, mortars and pestles, feathers, animal teeth, claws, pelts, and baskets.

For an exhibit on California tribes, consider the following specific touchables: acorns, Cream of Wheat™ (to simulate acorn meal), asphalt, abalone shells (bowls), bivalve shells (spoons), bear grass, flat-topped buckwheat, yucca, sage, laurel, and yerba santa.

From *Classroom Museums: Touchable Tables for Kids*, published by GoodYear Books. Copyright © 1992 Pamela Marx.

# Student Involvement in Table Preparation

Have students participate in exhibit preparation in several ways.

1. They can collect plants on nature walks to local parks, vacant lots, and nature centers. If you need to identify some of the plants you collect, a trip or phone call to a local nature center or park staffed by rangers and docents is helpful. You can use many of the plants and materials gathered for this table in the It's a Jungle Out There: Nature in Your Backyard exhibit as well.

2. Ask children to find things at home or in their yards that Native Americans might have used. These can include bivalve shells, small shells used as necklaces or beads, mortars and pestles, carved wooden bowls, maize, branches, rocks (which were heated and placed in baskets of mush to cook it), and similar items. Place these on your table with appropriate tags.

3. Children can sponge basket or textile designs common among local Native Americans onto the newsprint used to cover the exhibit table. Books on Native American life from the local or school library will have pictures of baskets and blankets decorated with traditional designs.

4. Have children make a pictograph (rock painting) or hide painting for the wall. Approach this in one of two ways. Ask them to research wall painting, hide painting, and rock art to learn about traditional designs. They can then re-create a design with markers or paints on a sheet of newsprint, tan-colored roll paper, or brown paper bag. Tear the edges to give it the look of rock or hide. If you use paper bag, "cure" it by dipping it in water, wringing it out and painting it with a wash of thinned brown paint. Or, children can brainstorm in groups to think of symbols they might use if they were living as the Native Americans did several hundred years ago. Have them make up short stories or messages using their picture symbols, such as "The sun rose over the big mountain. At noon, the people danced and the Great Spirit sent rain." The children should illustrate this "pictograph" with symbols for sun, rising sun, noon, mountain, dancers, and rain.

5. Students can make any village models you decide to include in the exhibit. Suggestions for creating these models are provided in the preceding section.

From *Classroom Museums: Touchable Tables for Kids*, published by GoodYear Books. Copyright © 1992 Pamela Marx.

*The text for this table differs slightly from that provided for other tables. Obviously, any exhibit of local Native American life will require some text materials or tags tailored to your particular locale. It is not possible to include so many diverse stories here, so instead, this text provides background information about Native Americans in each of five regions. This material does not go into any detail about local plants and lifeways.*

*The text on early California peoples demonstrates how to create your own geographically based label copy. It is not particularly long, but even a text of this length and specificity can be enlightening to children. It shows how native peoples who lived where the children live made use of everything, wasted nothing, and took nothing for granted.*

## Introduction

### Native Americans in Touch with the Land

Native Americans of North America adapted to climate, geologic formations, plants, animals and other resources available to them in the places they lived. These factors dictated the types of homes they built, the clothes they wore and the foods they ate. Many individual groups or nations of Native Americans lived in different parts of North America. Sometimes several nations whose territories bordered one another would forge an alliance. These groups spoke a common language. The information here focuses primarily on how Native Americans of North America survived and prospered before their lifestyles were affected by settlers and colonists from Europe.

## The Southeast

### Native Americans of the Southeast

Many Native American groups lived in the Southeast. Each group was divided into clans. The different clans had many things in common even though they lived all over a large area of land that included what is now called Florida, Tennessee, Mississippi, and Alabama.

The Southeast is an area with diverse plant life. Native Americans gathered many local plants for food. Some of the plants they ate were wild fruit, pumpkins, and squash. The Choctaw of Mississippi and Alabama and the Seminole of Florida also ate nuts, seeds, roots, and beans. Some groups cultivated vegetables, primarily corn.

Most tribes also hunted small game with bows and arrows, clubs, or blow guns. Some groups had access to larger game like buffalo and deer. Those who lived near the shore fished for food as well.

Tribes built different kinds of homes depending upon the resources available to them. Seminole from the Florida area, for example, lived in *chickees*. These were simple shelters consisting largely of grass or palm leaf roofs on wooden poles.

Tattooing was a common practice among many of these early southeasterners. The warriors (those who were the best hunters) earned the honor of the tattoo. Tattooing was done with a cactus spine needle and ink made from charred wood.

From *Classroom Museums: Touchable Tables for Kids*, published by GoodYear Books. Copyright © 1992 Pamela Marx.

The Cherokee were the largest of the southeastern groups. They lived in the Tennessee area in villages ruled by a chief and a council of wise men. Each year they held a festival when their corn ripened. Sequoya was a famous Cherokee leader who created an alphabet for the Cherokee language so that his people could learn to read and write.

The Seminole lived in the Florida everglades. They developed a shallow canoe for traveling in the waters of the everglades. To hunt deer, they covered themselves with deerskins so that they could get very close before attacking. They used the deer for everything. They ate the meat. From the skin they made moccasins and clothing. The antlers made good tools. They used the sinews of the muscles for thread.

# The Northeast

## Native Americans of the Northeast

The Native Americans of the Northeast lived in the areas now known as New York, Delaware, New Jersey, Pennsylvania, Maine, Rhode Island, Massachusetts, and Connecticut. These groups lived in several different types of houses. A typical shelter was the longhouse. These were often covered with bark.

The northeastern groups collected food from many sources. Many of them cultivated crops like corn. They also gathered plants, berries, fruits, nuts, and seeds. They hunted a wide variety of local game like deer, elk, geese, and turkey. The lakes and oceans were full of fish. Some of these groups also collected maple sap for syrup.

The birch tree was very important to many of the northeastern groups. They used its bark to cover their houses. Some used it for making baskets, cooking containers, and canoes.

Two alliances of Native American nations in the Northeast were the Iroquois and the Algonquian. The Onondaga, Mohawk, Cayuga, Tuscarora, Oneida, and Seneca were part of the Iroquois group. The Iroquois were experienced farmers and many of their religious ceremonies centered around agriculture and harvest.

The Algonquian group also included many individual tribes. The Delaware tribe was one of the most important tribes of this group. The men of the tribe did the building, hunting, and fishing while the women gathered and cooked the food. The Wampanoag assisted the Pilgrims and taught them how to grow corn. These Native Americans used shells from the shellfish they ate in many ways. They made them into beads and used them for barter (trade). They fashioned jewelry from tiny periwinkle shells. The Pennacook made tools and weapons from clam and turtle shells, wood, bark, and stones. They made ornaments from fish bones and animal horns.

From *Classroom Museums: Touchable Tables for Kids*, published by GoodYear Books. Copyright © 1992 Pamela Marx.

## Native Americans of the Plains

After the tribes of the Great Plains learned to domesticate and use horses, they rode from place to place in search of buffalo. The availability of horses enlarged their hunting grounds and changed their ways of life. They traveled more. They farmed less.

They relied on the buffalo for many things including food, clothing, and coverings for their tepees. Most of the Plains tribes lived in tepees, but some did not. The Pawnee lived in earthen lodges. The Osage lived in rectangular houses covered with skins.

While the Plains tribes were primarily buffalo hunters, some also harvested crops for food. The Pawnee of the Nebraska and Kansas areas, for example, planted crops. After planting, they left them to grow while they went on long buffalo hunts. They returned later to harvest the crops.

Many of the Plains tribes migrated to the central Great Plains from other parts of North America. The Cheyenne moved from Minnesota to the Black Hills of South Dakota and into the Great Plains. As they moved, they changed from corn farmers to buffalo hunters. They also enjoyed games. They played games like stick in the hoop, kickball, and a game similar to field hockey.

Many call the Dakota (also known as the Sioux) the great culture of the Plains. The Dakota were known for their resistance to settlers. Famous leaders such as Sitting Bull and Crazy Horse were members of the Dakota tribe.

The Comanche lived in the Texas and Oklahoma areas. They were nomadic (wandering) buffalo hunters and excellent horse handlers. They waged a forty-year war against Texas settlers because they resented them taking away the best hunting grounds.

## Native Americans of the Northwest

Several interesting traditions distinguish the Native Americans of the Northwest. One is the craft of the totem pole. Totem poles are large logs carved with animal images. The poles and the images they bear tell about the family that carved them and that family's history. Pole carving styles and particular animals represent certain clans. The northwestern groups also carve boxes, masks, and utensils from wood.

Another feature of the Northwest cultures was a practice called the *potlatch*. Potlatches were great feasts attended by guests from other clans. Clans hosted potlatches to celebrate happy events such as weddings or births. The host clan gave each guest a gift. Often the guest clan then invited the hosts back to a feast put on by their clan. These gifts and feasts were symbols of status.

The Native Americans of the Northwest include the Haida, Tlingit, Tsimshian, and Kwakiutl, among many others. Those groups who lived on the coast or by rivers harpooned whales or fished for salmon. They cooked whale blubber down into oil and used it for fuel, lamp oil, and to preserve food. They also used fish oils. Fishing clans traded fish for furs collected by hunting clans.

Many groups built large shelters from red cedar trees. Several families usually shared a shelter. The people made many utensils and household items such as baskets, dishes, mats, ropes, and clothing from parts of the cedar tree.

Alaskan tribes such as the Eskimo, Tlingit, and Aleut may have originally come from Greenland. They came to the Northwest later than some of the other groups. These people were fishers and hunters. They used animal skins, wood, bark, and bones to meet their daily needs. Some used large ice blocks to make their homes. Some wove bird feathers together to make beautiful capes and blankets.

From *Classroom Museums: Touchable Tables for Kids*, published by GoodYear Books. Copyright © 1992 Pamela Marx.

# Native Americans of the Southwest

Many thousands of years ago, a land bridge existed between Asia and North America. Groups of people crossed the land bridge as they hunted food and game for survival. That area is now a body of water called the Bering Strait.

Some of these people left the Northwest and began moving south. Perhaps long droughts killed off large game animals, and they moved south to find more and better food sources. Their lives changed in the mild southern climate. They hunted small game and gathered wild plants. They needed limited clothing. Many lived in grass-covered huts and wove baskets from local grasses and plants.

In this new, warmer climate, life became less nomadic. Some groups of people began to farm corn, squash, and/or beans. Farming meant people needed to stay in one place. As a result, village life became common.

Many of these southwesterners are now called Puebloans. Some of the many tribes within this large group are the Hopi, Zuni, and Acoma.

Many Pueblo villages have similar structures and plans. Often, in the center of the village was a ceremonial chamber called a *kiva*. It was used for important rituals and religious events. Other village structures and shelters surrounded the kiva. The Pueblo groups built flat-topped shelters from adobe. Some southwestern groups built their adobe dwellings in caves. They developed elaborate villages in the walls of cliffs and mountains.

The Pima of the Arizona area carved wooden implements for farm tools. They grew cotton, which they then wove into cloth for clothing and other daily needs.

The Papago notched sticks to use as calenders. They carved the notches in different patterns. If you used notches on a stick to keep track of time, what would your notches stand for and what notching design would you use? Would you carve one notch for each sunrise? Would you carve one notch for each full moon?

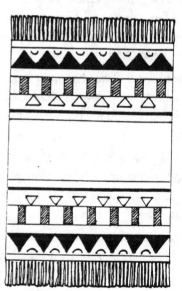

The Navajo are one of the largest tribes in the United States. They were a nomadic group that entered the Southwest quite late compared to other groups. The Spanish explorers brought sheep and horses to the area. As a result, the Navajo began to raise sheep and use the wool for making cloth, rugs, and blankets. They are famous for their weaving and design skills.

The Apache are another Southwestern tribe. They, like the Navajo, arrived late to the southwestern area and were a nomadic group.

From *Classroom Museums: Touchable Tables for Kids*, published by GoodYear Books. Copyright © 1992 Pamela Marx.

The Native Americans of the Southwest have had many forms of expression throughout the years. One that they shared with Native Americans all over North America was "writing" stories and relating tribal events and religious practices by carving or painting them on cave walls or cliff faces. Many of these images can still be seen in the Southwest. The carvings are called *petroglyphs*. The paintings are called *pictographs*.

Pottery is another craft common among Native Americans of the Southwest. Different groups developed distinctive techniques and designs.

The Navajo use sandpainting in religious rituals. These designs made with sand on the ground are destroyed immediately after the ceremony ends. The Hopi make kachina dolls to represent helping spirits and to help teach Hopi culture to the people.

*[The remainder of the text illustrates how to develop information about the Native Americans of a specific geographic area. This particular text focuses on groups in the southern California area.]*

## California Native Americans and Their Environment

**California**

At one time, a hundred different Native American groups inhabited California. Those in the southern California area included the Chumash and Gabrielino peoples. Both of these groups were excellent artisans skilled in basket-making, boat-making, and stone carving.

Living near the coast, the Chumash were the most sea-oriented Native Americans in California. They developed plank canoes, which they steered in ocean waters with double-bladed paddles, and became skilled at fishing. Their boats took them to the nearby Channel Islands where they found steatite, which they used for carving stone cooking pots.

The Native Americans who lived in the southern California area over two hundred years ago were like all Native American peoples in their respect for the land on which they lived. They took from the land only what they needed. They made use of all the natural resources around them. They hunted animals for food, not for sport. Animal skin served as clothing and blankets, and bone as tools and decoration. Plants were in good supply. They used them for food, medicines, baskets, soap, clothing, housing, bedding, and diapers. This exhibit will help you see how creatively Native Americans used the materials available to them.

From *Classroom Museums: Touchable Tables for Kids*, published by GoodYear Books. Copyright © 1992 Pamela Marx.

From *Classroom Museums: Touchable Tables for Kids*, published by GoodYear Books. Copyright © 1992 Pamela Marx.

## Oak Trees

*Several different varieties of oak grew in California. The people made use of whatever type of oak grew nearby.*

### Oak Trees **Acorns**

The seed of an oak is called an *acorn*. The acorn was one of the most important foods eaten by California people. They ground acorns with a *pestle,* or grinding tool, on a mortar. A *mortar* was a deep indentation or hole in a rock. A basket over the mortar kept the ground meal from flying out during the crushing process.

Raw acorns are bitter and do not make good eating. Native Americans removed the bitterness from the acorns by mashing them and running water over them. Once the acorns were ground and *leached* in this way, they were used as food. Dry acorn meal looks a lot like Cream of Wheat™. Most people preferred to eat it mixed with water and cooked into a mush that also tasted like Cream of Wheat™. The soupy mush might be eaten from an abalone shell bowl with a spoon made of a clam shell, carved wood, or antler. Sometimes acorn meal would be mixed with a little water and baked into a cake, but this was less common.

People collected acorns from oak trees in the fall and stored them in granaries for winter eating. These granaries were built on stilts of strong stalks and covered with grasses to protect the acorns from weather and animals.

### Oak Trees **Other Uses of Oak**

People used the wood of the oak tree to carve bowls and other eating utensils, the ashes of burnt oak to mix medicine, and oak bark to make brown dye for clothing and basket weaving.

## Bear Grass

### Bear Grass **Roots**

The roots of bear grass were eaten.

### Bear Grass **Stems/Leaves**

The grass itself was used as cord for making tightly woven baskets.

## Juniper

*This evergreen plant had several uses.*

### Juniper **Berries**

The berries from the juniper plant were used in food and drink. Even today juniper berries are used in cooking to flavor meat.

### Juniper **Roots**

The roots were used as fiber or cord for making baskets.

### Juniper **Branches**

The fragrant branches were used for making medicines. Larger pieces of wood made good hunting bows.

### Juniper **Bark**

Soft bark shavings could be stuffed into baby cradles as mattress and diapering material.

## Cattail

*This plant grows in wet, marshy areas. It had many important uses.*

### Cattail **Roots/Pollen**

These parts of the plant were used for food. Cattail roots provided a starchy energy source.

### Cattail **Stalks**

The tall, sturdy stalks of the cattail were used to make houses.

### Cattail **Flowers**

The soft material of the cattail flower was used for diapering babies and for mattress material in cradles. Mothers simply threw away the soiled cattails. Unlike the plastic diapers used today, "cattail diapers" decomposed naturally and did not pose a threat to the environment.

From *Classroom Museums: Touchable Tables for Kids*, published by GoodYear Books. Copyright © 1992 Pamela Marx.

From *Classroom Museums: Touchable Tables for Kids*, published by GoodYear Books. Copyright © 1992 Pamela Marx.

## Yucca

*This was a common plant in the California desert.*

### Yucca **Flowers/Stalks/Pods**

Yucca flowers, the flower stalks, and the fruit or seedpods, as well as other parts of the plant, were used for food.

### Yucca **Roots**

The roots were used to make soap. Young root shoots were used to make dyes.

### Yucca **Leaves**

Yucca leaves are large, flat, and full of fibers. The fibers in the leaves were used to make baskets. Nets, brushes, strings for bows, and sandals were also made from yucca leaves.

## Sunflowers

### Sunflowers **Seeds**

The native peoples ate sunflower seeds. Unlike the sunflower seeds we eat today, the wild seeds Native Americans ate did not have shells.

### Sunflowers **Roots**

Sunflower plant roots were used for making medicines.

While a major part of the California native diet was based upon the acorn, the people also ate many kinds of seeds and plants, some of which you will see in other parts of this table exhibit. They hunted deer, elk, bear, and rabbit, and they fished. Insects also were eaten; the local people might have dined on ants, bee larvae, aphids, and grasshoppers. After soaking in salt water, grasshoppers were roasted over hot rocks to prepare them for eating.

## Examples of Tag Text

*The following individual paragraphs are examples of tags that can be placed around your exhibit table to identify specific plants, utensils, touchables, or pictures that are not otherwise covered by your text. The labels commencing with "Chumash Village" specifically demonstrate how you can use pictures to augment the touchables in your exhibit.*

**Cleaned Chicken or Beef Bones**—Native Americans used bones from the animals they ate to make tools, clothing decorations, and musical instruments. Small bones might have been used to make necklaces or bird whistles.

**Feathers**—Some Native Americans used feathers from birds as clothing and basket decoration. The Plains tribes used large feathers to make huge headdresses that they wore as war bonnets.

**Shells**—Large shells were used as spoons and even bowls. Small shells were strung on necklaces for decoration or barter.

**Wood Logs**—People carved branches and logs to make bowls and utensils. Some tribes notched small sticks to keep track of time.

**Fibrous Plants such as Bear Grass (florists use this) and Yucca**—The people wove grasses and plants with strong fibers into baskets. Native Americans used baskets for many things including cooking, storage, and transporting. They sometimes waterproofed baskets with tar for carrying water.

**Cattails, mosses, wood shavings**—These items were used in cradles to "diaper" babies.

**Chumash Village**—This picture shows what a Chumash village might have looked like. This village was located on the beach. Notice how the huts are constructed of local plant material.

**Basket Weaving**—This woman is weaving a basket. She is sitting outside her hut. Her children are playing in the background.

**Granary**—Acorns grow on oak trees in October. The Native Americans collected all the acorns they could during their growing season and stored them in granaries such as the one pictured. Acorns could be stored in this way for up to two years.

**Soapstone Bowl**—This is a picture of a soapstone bowl used by the Chumash. Soapstone is a natural stone that can be heated for cooking purposes without breaking. The Chumash and Gabrielino people carved this stone into pots and griddles. Soapstone (also known as *steatite*) comes from Catalina Island.

**Cooking Acorn Mush**—These people are cooking acorn mush by boiling dry acorn meal in water heated by hot rocks. The mush cooks as quickly this way as our modern hot cereals cook on a stove.

**Mortar**—This picture shows a grinding stone (mortar) used to grind acorns and other plant seeds into meal. A smaller stone (pestle) was rubbed against the larger stone to mash and grind the seeds which people collected.

**Planked Canoe**—A planked canoe is pictured here. The Chumash made and used such canoes in ocean fishing. Those who lived near rich petroleum deposits used the tar and asphalts they found to help waterproof their boats and baskets. They also used tar to plug holes in large seashells that they used as bowls.

## Native American Legends

Beginning at the reference desk at your local library, research Native American legends about your community. Some of these legends may be about local natural landmarks. Consider the following example.

From *Classroom Museums: Touchable Tables for Kids*, published by GoodYear Books. Copyright © 1992 Pamela Marx.

## The Legend of the Eagle Rock—A Gabrielino Legend

*Eagle Rock is the landmark for which the community of Eagle Rock in Los Angeles is named. The Native Americans who lived near the rock had a legend to explain how the eagle got into the rock. It goes like this:*

A family lived by the rock. They had a small baby. The mother ground acorns. The father gathered berries and nuts. The other children played with the village dog. One day as the family worked and played in the sun, an eagle swooped down and carried the baby skyward. The family was shocked and frightened for the baby's safety. They called upon the Great Spirit to bring the eagle down and save the baby. When the Great Spirit heard the family's cry, he took pity. Suddenly, the eagle was unable to fly. He fell hard from the sky and crashed against the great rock by which the family lived. The baby fell to earth unharmed landing in the leaves of a laurel bush. To this day, when the sun shines brightly overhead, the eagle's shadow can be seen in the great rock.

## Discussion Guidelines

*The guidelines provided here do not assume a particular geographic area. They are generic questions intended to start discussion and spark creative thinking about Native American ways of life. They will challenge students to think about what Native American life might have been like two hundred years ago. What would students do to survive the elements?*

### Locale

In what kind of land did the people live?

*Mountainous    Desert    Woodland*
*Snow covered    Coastal    Swamp*

What is the weather/climate like?

*Hot    Cold    Dry*
*Rainy    Temperate versus seasonal change*

What kinds of animals live in the area now and several hundred years ago?

What kind of plant life abounds?

### Clothing

What kind of clothing would you use in warm weather?

*Limited clothing*
*Hunting tribes used skins around the waist.*
*Those who farmed cotton wove lightweight clothing.*
*Those who raised sheep wove woolen clothing.*
*Bark clothing*

What kind of clothing would you use in cold weather?

*Robes of animal skin or fur*
*Capes of tightly woven bird feathers (Alaska)*
*Seal fur*
*Heavily woven clothing/wool blankets*

### Shelter

What kind of shelter would you use in warm climates?

*Open huts/chickees, palm or grass roof supported by sticks (Southeast)*
*Dome-shaped grass huts (West/California)*
*Cliff dwellings (Southwest)*
*Adobe pueblos (Southwest)*
*Grass-branch-twig huts/wickiups (Southwest)*
*Easy to move tepees (Plains)*

What kind of shelter would you use in cold climates?

*Ice houses/igloos (Far North)*
*Wooden plank houses (Northwest)*
*Longhouses/wooden structures covered with skin or bark (Northeast)*
*Sod house reinforced with branches and twigs (Plains)*

### Food

How would you obtain food in warm weather?

What would you be able to eat?

*Hunt animals*
*Small animals like rabbit, squirrel, turkey, birds*
*Large animals like elk, caribou, deer, buffalo, moose*

How would you hunt?

*Bow and arrow*
*Clubs*
*Spears*
*Blow guns*
*Fish for fish and shellfish*
*Gather seeds, nuts, berries, plants, roots*
*Farm beans, corn, and squash (Northeast) or corn (Plains/Southwest)*

What other resources would you have for food?

How would you obtain food in cold weather?

What would you be able to eat?

*Hunt animals when you find them*
*Dried animal meat from hunting season/jerky*
*Corn acorns, seeds etc. collected and saved from growing and gathering season*

From *Classroom Museums: Touchable Tables for Kids*, published by GoodYear Books. Copyright © 1992 Pamela Marx.

What would you use for tools?

*Wood—carved bowls and utensils, farm implements, bows*
*Shells—bowls, spoons*
*Stone—carved bowls, mortars and pestles, arrows*
*Antlers/Large Bones—carved utensils and tools*
*Bark/Wood—boats*

## Recreation

What other things did Native Americans make from materials around them?

*Musical instruments*
  *Skins for drumheads*
  *Sticks*
  *Deer hooves for rattles*
  *Gourd rattles*
*Clothing decoration*
  *Feathers*
  *Porcupine quillwork*
  *Small shells, necklaces*
  *Small bones, necklaces*
  *Paints from rocks and plants*

What would you do when you were not hunting, cooking, or making clothing, boats, or shelter?

*Play games*
*Participate in ceremonies/dances*
*Make music*

## Student Activities

1. The game of toss and catch was played in one form or another by Native Americans from Alaska to Mexico. To make this toy, Native Americans attached slender skin straps to a thin stick made out of bone. On the other end of the straps, they attached hollowed-out bones (rings). The game was played by trying to catch the hollow bones on the end of the stick to which they were attached. Re-create this toy using a dowel or unsharpened pencil (or tightly rolled and taped posterboard), a twenty-four-inch string, and a $2^{1}/_{2}$-inch square of tagboard with a one-inch hole in it (or a ring from a plastic six-pack holder). Tie one end of the string to one end of the pencil or dowel. Secure it with a dot of glue or tape. Tie the other end of the string to the tagboard through a hole you have punched into one corner or to the plastic ring, depending upon the materials you choose to use. Try to catch the ring on the stick.

2. Make permanent sandpaintings with your class. Grind colored chalk (or use powdered tempera paint) into bowls of salt until the salt is colored to your satisfaction. Make several bowls of different colors of salt "sand." Children should create designs with glue on pieces of construction paper. They then drizzle the salt over the glue and shake it off. Locate the different colors of sand at different stations. Have children make their pictures in stages. First, they do part of the picture in glue and color it at one color station. Then they do another part of the picture and color it at another color station. In this way the colored sands remain relatively pure and the children have sandpaintings with several distinct colors.

3. Using a cement block (the type used to make block walls) and a small, smooth (yet hard) rock, have children try to grind corn as Native Americans did. Even without a real mortar and pestle, this experience shows children how much work early peoples did to make their food. You can use uncooked popcorn for grinding.

4. Have children bring in twigs about $^{1}/_{4}$- to $^{1}/_{2}$-inch in diameter and eight to twelve inches long from which to make notched calendar sticks. Using markers, have children "notch" designs comprised of straight and diagonal lines, "x" marks, and the like. Before they start notching, they should think about what they want each mark to mean. Does a straight line stand for each sunrise? Does it stand for each day between the full moons? Are they marking the days on a hunting trip or until the corn is ripe? This exercise helps children understand the ways in which Native Americans kept in touch with their natural surroundings. Combine this activity with a writing exercise by having the children describe the hunting trip or growing season during which they carved their notched sticks.

5. Make Native American fry bread.

### Native American Fry Bread

In a mixing bowl, combine 2 cups flour, $^{1}/_{2}$ teaspoon salt, 4 teaspoons baking powder and $^{2}/_{3}$ cup water (warm, if possible). If it is too sticky to work with, add flour a little at a time until you can knead dough in your hands. Be sure to flour your hands first. Dust a board or your table with flour and pat out balls of dough until flat (about one quarter inch thick). Cut dough into one-by-three-inch strips of flat dough. Fry in hot oil at least one inch deep until light brown. Top with honey, powdered sugar, or sugar and cinnamon. Serve warm. Be sure to do this activity with parental help to avoid any safety problems with the hot oil. Adequate supervision is imperative.

From *Classroom Museums: Touchable Tables for Kids,* published by GoodYear Books. Copyright © 1992 Pamela Marx.

6. Make tea with herbs as Native Americans did. Often teas were used for medicinal purposes. Some excellent teas can be made with lemon grass and/or mint leaves. Your research into local plants may give you some ideas about plants you can boil into tea.

7. Make adobe. Adobe is made from clay soil mixed with grass or straw and bits of plant fiber, sand and water. Some southwestern Native Americans made homes out of adobe. Have children experiment to find out how to make good, strong adobe. Use old plastic butter or applesauce containers to make round adobe bricks. (Better yet, collect rectangular containers.) Try four different adobe combinations. If you have sand available, include one-quarter cup or so with each combination.

   One cup soil plus enough water to make a thick paste

   One cup soil plus a quarter cup dried grass clippings and enough water to make thick paste

   Three quarters cup soil, three eighths cup dried grass clippings, and enough water to make thick paste

   One half cup soil, one half cup dried grass clippings, and enough water to make a thick paste

   Press each mixture into a different container. Try to have containers of the same size. Let dry in sun. Did any brick crack? Is any brick crumbly? Which holds together best? Which seems strongest? How does the grass help the adobe? (It makes it strong and helps eliminate cracking.) This exercise can double as an earth science experiment.

8. To make cornhusk masks, see activity 7 in Chapter 5.

## Resources

1. Local park and nature centers are excellent sources of both information and speakers about local Native American life. Park rangers and docents are very knowledgeable about indigenous wild plants and how the Native Americans used them. They will probably have interesting stories about how different plants were used.

2. Local and state natural history museums and Native American museums often have staff who are well-versed in the lifeways of native peoples. These historians, curators, and docents may have valuable information to share with you about local cultures, and they may be able to direct you to other community resources.

3. Many interesting Native American legends have been published in recent years. They contain wonderful illustrations. If you are unable to find speakers who can talk about Native American life, perhaps an adult volunteer or your local librarian could present books or tell stories based on Native American legends.

   Just a few of the many excellent books available are:

   *Arrow to the Sun, A Pueblo Indian Tale by Gerald McDermot*t, published by Puffin Books (1977) (Caldecott Medal winner).

   *The Great Race of the Birds and Animals* (Cheyenne/ Sioux) by Paul Goble, published by Aladdin Books (1991).

   *Quillworker A Cheyenne Legend* by Terri Cohlene, published by Watermill Press (1990) as part of its Native American legends series. Ask your librarian or bookstore clerk about other books in this series.

   *The Legend of the Indian Paintbrush* by Tomie de Paola, published by G. P. Putnam's Sons (1988).

From *Classroom Museums: Touchable Tables for Kids*, published by GoodYear Books. Copyright © 1992 Pamela Marx.

Name_____ Date _____

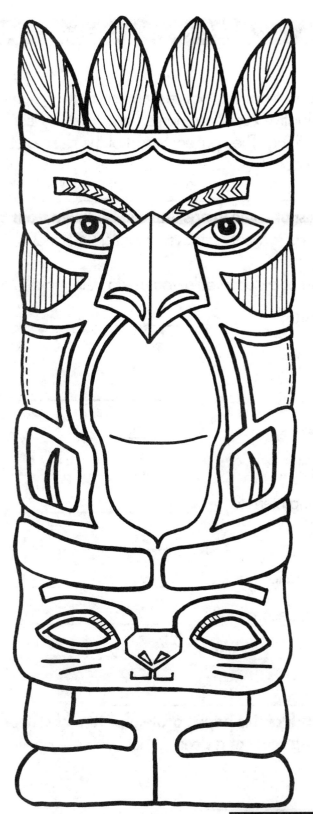

**Make your own totem pole.**
Color the animal designs.
Cut out pole design and
wings. Glue pole design
onto empty paper towel roll.
Fold wings on dotted line
and glue tab part of wings to
roll as part of bird design.

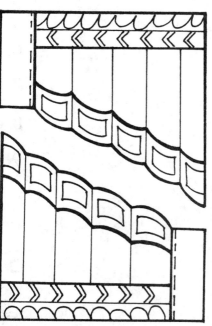

From *Classroom Museums: Touchable Tables for Kids*, published by GoodYear Books. Copyright © 1992 Pamela Marx.

**Using Prey**

Name_____ Date _____

## How did Native Americans use their prey?

Think about life for the Native Americans living hundreds of years ago. If a Native American hunted and killed a deer, he and his family wasted nothing. They put each part of the deer to use. What would you use a deer for?

**This is a list of some things that can be taken from a deer.**
Teeth • Hide • Meat • Hooves • Antlers • Bones

What part of a deer would you use to help make

1. a house? _____

2. a necklace? _____

3. food? _____

4. a rattle? _____

5. clothing? _____

6. an eating utensil? _____

7. a tool? _____

8. a drumhead? _____

9. clothing decoration? _____

**On the back of this paper, draw a picture of a necklace you might make using parts of a deer.** Would you use bones or hooves or teeth?

From *Classroom Museums: Touchable Tables for Kids*, published by GoodYear Books. Copyright © 1992 Pamela Marx.

# Sugar and Chocolate

*This exhibit takes children into the "how" and "why" world of some very familiar substances. Today, we take sugar and chocolate for granted, but not so long ago they were luxuries available only to the very wealthy.*

## Teacher Guidance

### Getting Started

The best way to start on this exhibit is to read the table text. You might decide to focus only on chocolate or only on sugar. Your local library may have a collection of books on the history of chocolate or sugar. Use these for additional background and to get ideas for visuals for your table.

Next, contact local or regional candy manufacturers to see what kinds of information and candy donations you can obtain.

Check with parents, friends, and students (especially those with strong ethnic ties) to see if they can help you collect an international variety of sweet treats. They might be able to give you information about candies and treats that are used for special holidays or ceremonies. See if any friends, parents, or community members make homemade candy like fudge, dipped chocolate, peanut brittle, or molded suckers. Demonstrations by these people will enhance your exhibit.

### Curriculum Integration

Integrate this subject into your curriculum in any of several ways.

1. **World Geography:** Sugar and chocolate have traveled all over the world. World geography can be taught or reinforced in conjunction with this exhibit, which provides a novel approach and deals with most of the major land masses.

2. **World History:** Sugary sweets and chocolate have been around throughout much of history. The Aztec civilization played an important role in the development of chocolate. The Middle East played a role in sugar. Sugar became an economic crop when it was grown with slave labor. These and other historical connections make this table a useful adjunct to a history curriculum.

3. **Nutrition:** Some people joke that junk food is a fifth food group. Any use of this table, whether by visit or sponsorship, dovetails with discussions of nutrition and food groups.

4. **Dental Hygiene:** The subject matter of this table almost demands discussion of the importance of dental hygiene.

5. **Physical Sciences:** A number of very good science experiments can be done with sugar. You can test the density of water with sugar. You can show crystal formation by making rock candy. You can demonstrate a physical change by making the candy recipe listed in the Student Activities section of this chapter.

*From Classroom Museums: Touchable Tables for Kids*, published by GoodYear Books. Copyright © 1992 Pamela Marx.

This exhibit should be divided into two parts. One part focuses on chocolate, the other on sugar. On the chocolate side of the table, arrange touchables from their rawest form to their most processed. If you can't obtain cacao beans, begin with pictures of pods and seeds. Then, display squares of baking chocolate, cocoa powder, and dehydrated milk. Cocoa powder might be interesting for children to taste since it is so bitter. It helps them understand the transformation of chocolate from a spiced, bitter Aztec drink to the sweet substance we know today. The next part of the table should include examples of molded chocolate candy bars, syrup, gold-covered coins and chips, chocolate molds, and candy-making forks, spoons, or other paraphernalia.

On the sugar side of the table, try to include a piece of sugar cane. Cane is available from time to time in local markets. Check with your produce grocer. This section can also incorporate various forms of sugar—granulated, powdered, brown, raw, and molasses. Include examples of other sweeteners (corn syrup, maple sugar).

Next, assemble as many different types of candy as you can locate: rock candy, candy corn, jelly beans, candy-covered almonds, mints, shaped suckers. Try to find examples that reflect different seasons, holidays, and cultures. Place your candies in small bowls or plates. Label or tag each sample with the name and where, how, and when it is used or eaten.

On the wall, mount a world map to show the travels of chocolate and sugar.

From *Classroom Museums: Touchable Tables for Kids*, published by GoodYear Books. Copyright © 1992 Pamela Marx.

## Sample Touchables

Most of the touchables for this exhibit will be easy to find, including cocoa powder, dehydrated milk, baking chocolate, chocolate chips, chocolate bars, candy molds, granulated sugar, sugar cubes, sugarcane, corn syrup, maple syrup, molasses, *mole* sauce (chocolate sauce for meat made in Mexico), gingerbread houses and other candy creations, jelly beans, candy-covered almonds, holiday candy (molded chocolate turkeys, pumpkin suckers, peppermint sticks, candy corn), photographs of the candy-making process (both current and historical), candy-making molds and tools. Cacao pods, cacao beans, sugar beets and candy company photographs might be harder to find but will add an interesting dimension to your table.

## Student Involvement in Table Preparation

Involve students in creating this exhibit in the following ways.

1.  Ask students to bring in unique samples of molded, holiday, or special interest candy for the exhibit. Any candy unique to a particular culture is especially good. Students can also bring in samples of cocoa powder, baking chocolate, or candy molds they have at home.

2.  Involve children in the making of a small gingerbread house. Decorate it with candies ranging from nonpareils to hard candy. Perhaps a student and his or her family would like to adopt this part of the table and complete it at home. Even a "gingerbread" house made from graham crackers is useful for display.

3.  The touchables for this table are limited and simple. Let children play a primary role in setting up the exhibit.

From *Classroom Museums: Touchable Tables for Kids*, published by GoodYear Books. Copyright © 1992 Pamela Marx.

**Table Text**

*This table text is comprised of two sections. One concerns chocolate and the other concerns sugar. You may choose to do your exhibit on only one subject, especially if you have a number of exhibit speakers and demonstration opportunities on that subject.*

## Sweet Dreams: Making and Using Sugar and Chocolate

*When people like chocolate and candies, we say they have a "sweet tooth." Some people say they crave chocolate. Others say they can't live without jelly beans. Since candies and chocolate are foods about which we have such definite opinions, let's find out more about them.*

# The History and Uses of Chocolate

*Chocolate is made from cacao beans that grow around the globe on cacao trees. These slender trees reach heights of twenty-five to forty feet. They have leathery leaves and bear fruit and seeds in pods called cacao pods. Ripe pods are slender and grow to about one foot in length. The pods are ribbed and woody looking. Each pod contains about twenty-five white to lavender seeds. These seeds are scooped out and used to make chocolate.*

## How Did Chocolate Become so Popular?

The great civilizations of Mexico were among the early users of chocolate. Both the Aztec and Mayan civilizations used cacao beans in many ways. The ancient people thought the beans were a special gift from the gods and treated them with great reverence. They used the beans in religious ceremonies, often prepared in a special beverage. Sometimes they used them as money.

About four hundred years ago, the history of chocolate changed forever. The year was 1519. Explorers from Spain, including a famous explorer named Cortez, watched Aztec king Montezuma II preside over a ceremony. During the ceremony, Montezuma presented Cortez with a gold goblet filled with a special brown drink. Cortez asked what it was. The Aztecs told him it was called *chocolatl*. It was very bitter because the Aztecs used no sugar. Instead, they whipped cacao beans with hot water and flavored the liquid with vanilla, pepper, and other spices. The Aztecs considered the liquid so precious that, once empty, the golden goblet that held it was tossed into a lake. After the ceremony, Montezuma showed Cortez the orchards of cacao trees that the Aztecs cultivated. Cortez saw how they fermented the cacao seeds or beans and ground them into a paste. They combined the paste with spices and hot water to make the frothy, brown beverage that Cortez had tasted.

When Cortez brought the cacao bean back to Spain, he taught the king and queen to mix the ground beans with vanilla, green pepper, and spices in hot water. While the Spanish drank chocolate like this for a while, they soon experimented by adding sugar. With this addition, the chocolate drink became very popular.

The Spanish guarded the secret of chocolate for over a hundred years. As a result, only royalty and very wealthy people had the chance to drink it. But word of chocolate spread. Some say that in 1606 an Italian who visited Spain got the recipe for the chocolate drink and took it home. He made it for his family and friends, and the secret of chocolate was out.

From *Classroom Museums: Touchable Tables for Kids*, published by GoodYear Books. Copyright © 1992 Pamela Marx.

Dutch and British explorers visited South America during this same period. There, too, they found cacao beans. They brought them back to Europe as Cortez and Columbus before him had done.

Wherever people tasted chocolate mixed with sugar, they liked it. Chocolate traveled to Austria and the rest of Europe. In each country, people responded enthusiastically.

King Louis XIV in France was one of chocolate's wealthy and powerful fans. It is said that his wife, a Spanish princess, gave chocolate to him as an engagement gift. In these early years, when only the wealthy could buy chocolate, it became a mark of success. Prosperous customers asked silversmiths and porcelain makers to craft elaborate pitchers and cups for serving chocolate.

By 1765, chocolate returned to America with the colonists. In Massachusetts, a man named John Hanan saw its potential. He asked Dr. John Baker to help him start a chocolate manufacturing operation. Their product is known today as baking chocolate. You can still find it in your grocery store. It is used in cooking chocolate desserts and treats.

Cacao Beans

## Where Do Cacao Beans Grow?

There are several different kinds of cacao trees. The beans from each have different flavors. Chocolate makers often combine the beans from different trees to make their chocolate products taste unique or special.

Cacao trees grow in parts of the world located within twenty degrees north or south of the equator. Parts of Africa and Central and South America are within these regions. They have warm climates and about forty-five inches of rain a year. Cacao trees need both warm weather and lots of water.

Some of the countries that have grown cacao beans are Ceylon, Madagascar, Brazil, Guatemala, Nigeria, Ghana, Ivory Coast, Colombia, and Ecuador. West African countries began growing cacao trees in the early 1900s. For many years, these countries have produced the majority of cacao beans grown in the world.

From *Classroom Museums: Touchable Tables for Kids*, published by GoodYear Books. Copyright © 1992 Pamela Marx.

From *Classroom Museums: Touchable Tables for Kids*, published by GoodYear Books. Copyright © 1992 Pamela Marx.

### How Are the Beans Processed?

Some fruits are picked before they ripen. This is not so with cacao beans. The pods ripen on the tree. When ripe, they are picked and cut open and the small beans inside removed. At this stage the beans are 60 percent water. The harvested beans are piled up, covered, and allowed to ferment for several days. They are then dried to remove excess moisture. Once these steps are completed, the beans are ready for inspection, bagging, and shipment.

When the beans arrive at the chocolate factory, they are fire roasted. As they roast, the inner bean, called the nib, shrinks and the shell begins to crack. When roasting is completed, the beans go to a winnowing machine. In this machine, the shell is cracked completely off the nib and husk material around the nib is blown away.

The nib is used to make chocolate. It is about one half cocoa butter. After winnowing, the roasted nibs are ground. During grinding, the cocoa butter is released turning the nibs into a thick dark liquid called *chocolate liquor*.

If the manufacturer makes cocoa powder, the chocolate liquor is pressed to squeeze out the cocoa butter. A hard cocoa cake is left behind. This is used to make cocoa powder.

If the manufacturer makes chocolate bars, the process is different. The chocolate liquor is mixed with sugar, more cocoa butter, and flavorings. If the manufacturer makes milk chocolate, dehydrated milk is also added at this stage. The mixture is then a thick paste.

Next, this chocolate paste is pressed again. This time the pressing is done through a roller system called a *refiner*. This process grinds remaining small particles until the texture of the chocolate is very smooth.

The refined chocolate paste goes into the *conch*, or kneading machine. In it, the chocolate is mixed over and over again. Sometimes this process goes on for days.

With conching complete, the chocolate is ready to be molded. It can be shaped into bars, chips, and flakes. Before shipping, the chocolate is aged much like cheese. This means the chocolate sits in a temperature-controlled area for a given period of time. Milk chocolate is aged for only a few weeks before shipment. It does not last as long as dark chocolate and is best when eaten within the first few months of manufacture. Dark chocolate is aged from three to six months and can even be aged for years to improve its taste.

## The History and Uses of Sugar

*Today, people in many countries take the availability of sugar for granted. They eat candies, cakes, pies, and pastries, most of which rely in good part on sugar for their taste. In recent years, scientists have studied how people respond to sugar and sweet tastes. They think most people have a built-in liking for sweets. This probably accounts for sugar's popularity once it is introduced to a people or a culture.*

*Yet, despite the amount of sugar that we eat, what do we really know about it? Did people always eat lots of sugar? How is sugar made? From what is it made?*

*Many different kinds of substances have been and are now used to sweeten things. What we usually think of as sugar is white granules made either from sugarcane or sugar beets. But, this is just one of many substances that are used as sweeteners. Others include honey, corn syrup, grape juice, and maple syrup. But since most of the candies that abound in stores are made from cane or beet sugar, we will focus on the history and uses of this sweetener.*

Sugar and Chocolate

*Throughout much of sugar's history, it was obtained almost exclusively from sugarcane, a tall grass. It grows in tropical and warm, mild climates. Cuba, Brazil, and India are big producers of sugarcane. In the United States, sugar cane grows in Hawaii. Today, sugar is also produced from sugar beets. The roots of these beets produce the sugar. Sugar beets grow in more temperate climates. Russia, France, Germany, and the United States are large sugar beet producers.*

## What Do We Know About Sugar's Past?

Sugar has been around the world many times over. Historians believe that ancient people first grew sugarcane thousands of years ago. Some scholars think people first domesticated it in New Guinea and that it then spread to other places like the Philippines, India, and Indonesia.

Sugarcane and its product, sugar, probably arrived in Europe at some time during the early Middle Ages, although some historians think it may have been earlier. The Crusades helped spread its use throughout Europe. The Crusades were a series of wars between European Christians and Arab Moslems. The Arabs were experienced in the cultivation, production, and technology of sugar making. Contact between the Arabs and the Europeans during these wars ensured the introduction of sugar into many parts of Europe. Sugar then played a part in the development of trade between the East and the West.

Even after sugar was introduced into Europe, though, its use was very limited for hundreds of years. People used it mostly as a spice, like salt or pepper. Only the wealthy had access to it. Over the centuries, this changed dramatically.

Sugar's history in England is a good example of this change. It may have been introduced into England as early as A.D. 1000. Its use grew slowly. Since sugarcane grew only in certain climates, it had to be imported. Therefore, sugar (like chocolate) was a luxury enjoyed by very few. By 1650, sugar was a preferred treat of English nobles and wealthy families. They mixed it in tea. They added it to medicines. Possessing it meant importance. Poets began to refer to it in their poems. But even so, few common people in England could afford to buy or use sugar.

By 1800, all this had changed. People, regardless of rank, viewed sugar as a necessity. It remained rare and costly, but people of all classes tried to obtain it. It was used to sweeten bitter foods like tea, coffee, and chocolate. By 1900, one fifth of all calories consumed by the English were in sugar.

As sugar's tremendous popularity grew, so did the need to grow it in great quantities. Here lies part of sugar's bitter history. To grow sugarcane, many people must work the fields. As England and other European countries colonized tropical areas around the world, settlers established slave plantations. Sugarcane grew on some of these plantations in the New World. Europeans took people from Africa and forced them to work in the sugarcane fields as slaves.

The growing of sugarcane on New World plantations had its beginnings with Columbus. On Columbus's second journey to the Americas in 1493, he brought sugarcane with him from Spain to see how it would grow. It was first grown in the Western Hemisphere on the Spanish island of Santo Domingo. The first shipment left for Europe from there in 1516. The experiment, however, was not terribly successful. It took other efforts to make New World sugarcane production successful.

From *Classroom Museums: Touchable Tables for Kids*, published by GoodYear Books. Copyright © 1992 Pamela Marx.

## How Do People Use Sugar?

Today, sugar is available both from sugarcane and sugar beets. Since it is abundant, candies and sweetmeats requiring sugar are popular all over the world. People in some countries have a greater fondness for sugar products than people in other countries. For example, most Americans eat a lot of sugar. In Africa, though, sugar is a very small part of the average diet. Sugar candies have become important parts of holiday festivities, religious celebrations, and important family traditions in many parts of the world. Day of the Dead celebrations in Mexico bring out vendors loaded with sugar skulls. Candy-coated almonds symbolizing good luck are important favors for weddings in some countries. In the United States, Valentine's Day is a big candy holiday when stores feature candy cupids, chocolate hearts, and heart-shaped boxes of sugary and chocolate goodies.

## How Is Sugar Grown and Processed?

*Sucrose* is another name for sugar. It occurs in all green plants. It is actually the plant's food. It is manufactured by the plant through the process of *photosynthesis*. During this process, the plant uses sunlight to make sugar from carbon dioxide and water.

Some plants manufacture sugar in ways that make it more useful to people as food. Sugarcane is a very large grass. Enough sugar is stored in one stalk to make a tasty treat. You can enjoy the sweetness of sugarcane by simply cutting a stalk and chewing a piece of the inner fiber. In sugar beets, the sugar is concentrated in the bulb-shaped root.

Because sugarcane has been the primary source of sugar throughout history, and since the majority of sugar today is still made from sugar cane, let's see how sugar is extracted from the cane. After harvest, the cane is chopped. Workers then grind, press (or pound) it and soak it in liquid to get the sugar out of the fibers. Once the sweet liquid is separated from the cane, it is heated.

The heated liquid is a supersaturated solution of sugar and water. This is like heavy water. As the hot solution cools, it is placed in a vacuum pan or a centrifuge (machine that spins liquids to separate substances of different densities). Here the sugar crystallizes. Raw sugar crystals form and molasses, a dark, thick, bittersweet liquid, drains off. For many years, molasses was as important a sweetener in some countries as refined sugar. The crystals then go through refining processes to become the granulated, powdered, and brown sugar that we buy in the store.

From *Classroom Museums: Touchable Tables for Kids*, published by GoodYear Books. Copyright © 1992 Pamela Marx.

Sugar and Chocolate

## Discussion Guidelines

*The general discussion of candy and chocolate can be enhanced by presentations put on by parents or by students with adult help. Demonstrations can include making a gingerbread house, molding suckers, cooking fudge, and dipping chocolates. While candy making is largely mechanized today, such demonstrations show what a labor-intensive process it has traditionally been.*

What is your favorite candy?

How many of you like chocolate?

What kinds of chocolate do you like?

Can you think of two kinds that you often see?

> *Dark          Milk*

Why do you think milk chocolate is called by that name?

> *It contains milk, usually dry or dehydrated.*

Do you know what chocolate is made from?

> *It is made from cacao beans.*

Where do chocolate makers get these beans?

> *The beans grow in equatorial parts of the world where the climate is warm and wet.*

How do they grow?

> *On trees          In seed pods*
> *The beans are the seeds inside the pods.*

How do you make chocolate from these beans? The beans are:

For cocoa powder

> *Fermented     Roasted     Winnowed*
> *Ground        Pressed*

For chocolate bars

> *Fermented*
> *Roasted*
> *Winnowed*
> *Ground*
> *Mixed with cocoa butter, sugar, and flavorings*
> *Dry milk is added if making milk chocolate.*
> *Refined*
> *Conched*
> *Molded*

How did people start using chocolate as a sweet treat?

> *Spanish explorer Cortez brought chocolate to Spain from the Aztecs.*
> *It was prepared as a spiced hot drink.*
> *Spanish weren't crazy about it so they added sugar.*
> *With sugar, chocolate became very popular.*

Many people like sweet things. What things can you think of that are sweet?

> Of what are they made?

> > *Sugar, corn syrup, molasses, fructose, maple syrup*

From what is sugar made?

> > *Sugar cane—Tall sturdy grass*
> > *Sugar beets—Root*

What did people use for sweetener before sugar was so easily available?

> > *Pumpkin syrup—Pilgrims*
> > *Molasses—it was more available to pioneers than refined sugar.*

What do you do with sugar at home?

> > *Cookies          Cakes          Candy*

Look at granulated sugar. What does it look like?

> > *Tiny crystals    White*

Can you make it look different?

> > *Heat it.          Dissolve it in water.*

What happens if you heat it? Does it change? How does it change?

> > *Yes. It melts into a clear, thick, sticky substance. As it cooks, this substance turns brown.*

Making these changes happen and controlling them are the candy maker's job.

What kinds of candies are made from sugar?

> > *Jelly beans, butterscotch, gummy candy*

Even the foods and treats we eat become part of the culture in which we live. They come to symbolize certain events and traditions. Do you buy or use special kinds of candy for different holidays or festivities?

> > *Chocolate hearts for Valentine's Day*
> > *Candy-coated almonds for weddings*
> > *Mints for weddings*
> > *Candy corn for Halloween*

What candies do you like best?

*From Classroom Museums: Touchable Tables for Kids, published by GoodYear Books. Copyright © 1992 Pamela Marx.*

1.  Make candied walnuts. The process of making this candy is really a science experiment. It shows the students how sugar changes from its opaque crystal state when heated and how it returns to a hard opaque state when cooled.

### Candied Walnuts

To make candied walnuts you need 1½ cup sugar, ½ cup liquid, 1 teaspoon light corn syrup, ¼ teaspoon salt, and 2½ cups walnuts or pecans. The liquid used can be orange juice, milk with ½ teaspoon mint flavoring, or water with ½ teaspoon cinnamon. Combine all ingredients except nuts in a two quart saucepan. Heat over medium heat until the mixture reaches 238 degrees. Measure this with a candy thermometer clipped to the side of the pan. This should take about five minutes. Turn off heat and add nuts. Stir until dry. This will take several minutes of constant stirring. Use a large wooden spoon. As you stir, the mixture changes from clear to opaque. It then dries onto the nuts.

Other science experiments with sugar include making rock candy (crystal formation), adding sugar to water (water density), and taste-bud testing (sweet, salty, sour, bitter).

2.  Make chocolate candy suckers for a special holiday, a classroom treat, or a class fundraiser. Locate a local party shop, department store, or candy supply shop that sells plastic chocolate sucker molds. Ask parents if they have any molds at home. Many parents, especially those involved with youth groups, have invested in sucker molds.

### Chocolate Candy Suckers

Have enough plastic chocolate sucker molds to make a sucker for each child or plan to do the project in groups of six to eight students at a time. Buy sucker or popsicle sticks. Melt chocolate chips over low heat in a double boiler. Place the sucker sticks in the molds and pour melted chocolate over them. Refrigerate and pop out suckers. If you make the suckers with a few students at a time, cool each set of suckers between groups. This can work smoothly with parental help if you have an ice chest with a bag of ice to "refrigerate" each mold as it is completed. This shortens the time it takes for suckers to harden and pop out so you can use the mold again.

3.  Make almond bark.

### Almond Bark

Melt a twelve ounce bag of chocolate chips. For a marbled effect, melt six ounces of chocolate chips and six ounces of white chocolate chips. Lay out one cup of almonds on a greased cookie sheet. Pour the melted chips over the almonds. Cool and then break into pieces of candy "bark."

### Peanut Clusters

Have children place six to eight dry roasted peanuts together on waxed paper. Drizzle a spoonful of melted chocolate over each cluster. Let cool.

4.  Another easy candy to make is peanut clusters.

From *Classroom Museums: Touchable Tables for Kids*, published by GoodYear Books. Copyright © 1992 Pamela Marx.

## Resources

1. A small local candy-making operation may be delighted to send a representative to talk about the candy-making process and/or to demonstrate it. Such an effort is advertising for the candy maker, especially if you have a school newsletter in which you can publish a thank you.

2. Some larger candy companies may have donation departments. These departments may be able to help you with brochures or materials that describe the candy-making process or the history of some of their most famous treats. You might ask the bigger companies listed here for candy donations or pictures. Even a brochure with a few pictures can be helpful. (There is no guarantee that these companies have any formal donations policies. However, this list is a good starting point for your research.) Perhaps a parent or your class could write letters to some candy companies requesting help. Direct them to the public relations/donations departments.

Hershey Food Corporation
    19 E. Chocolate Avenue
    Hershey, PA 17033
    717-534-4200

Ghirardelli Chocolate Company
    1111 139th Avenue
    San Leandro, CA 94578
    415-483-6970

See's Candy Shops, Inc.
    3423 South La Cienaga Boulevard
    Los Angeles, CA 90016
    213-870-3761

Russell Stover Candies Inc.
    100 Walnut Street
    Kansas City, MO 64106
    816-842-9240

Fannie May Candy Shops Inc.
    1137 West Jackson Boulevard
    Chicago IL 60607
    312-243-2700

Guittard Chocolate Company
    10 Guittard Road
    Burlingame, CA 94010
    415-697-4427

Fanny Farmer Candy Shops Inc.
    5885 Grant Avenue
    Cleveland, Ohio 44105
    216-883-9700

Nestle Company, Inc.
    100 Manhattanville Road
    Purchase, NY 10577
    914-251-3000

Whitman's Chocolates
    Division of Pet, Inc.
    P.O. Box 6070
    Philadelphia, PA 19114
    215-464-6000

From *Classroom Museums: Touchable Tables for Kids*, published by GoodYear Books. Copyright © 1992 Pamela Marx.

From *Classroom Museums: Touchable Tables for Kids*, published by GoodYear Books. Copyright © 1992 Pamela Marx.

**From Cacao Bean to Chocolate Bar**

Name_____ Date _____

**Place sentences about chocolate in the right order:**

Cacao beans are ground.                                                      1

Chocolate liquor is mixed with sugar, cocoa butter,                          2
and flavorings.

Cacao beans are harvested from cacao pods.                                   3

Chocolate is molded into desired shape.                                      4

Cacao beans are fermented, roasted, and winnowed.                           5

**The Early Travels of Chocolate**

From *Classroom Museums: Touchable Tables for Kids*, published by GoodYear Books. Copyright © 1992 Pamela Marx.

Name_____ Date _____

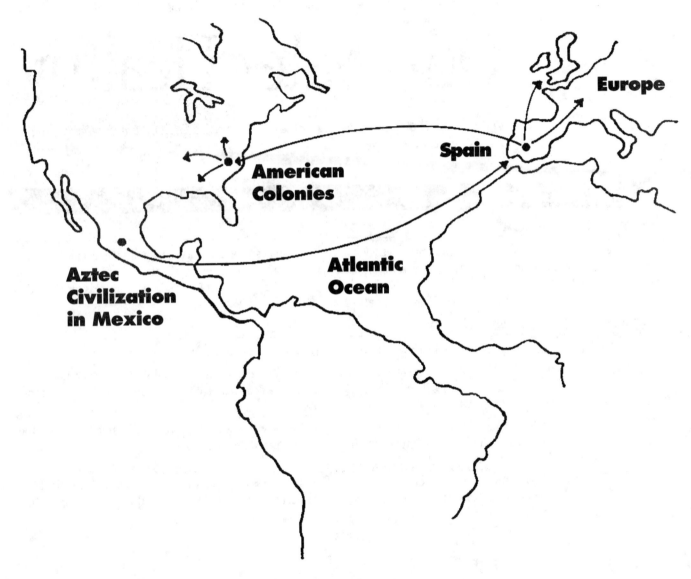

1. The Aztecs used chocolate in _____.

2. Cortez took chocolate to _____.

3. Chocolate use spread throughout _____.

4. Chocolate use then crossed the Atlantic Ocean to the _____ colonies.

# Keeping Our Earth, Our Air, Our Water Healthy

*This environmental table is suitable for use in conjunction with Earth Day or other environmental awareness activities.*

## Teacher Guidance

### Getting Started

Read the table text before you begin. This gives you an idea of possible subjects to cover and helps you decide how to focus your environmental efforts. Next, you might want to peruse one of the many excellent children's environmental handbooks. (See the Resources section of this chapter for suggestions.) These books give wonderful ideas for children's environmental awareness activities. They might also give you touchable ideas.

### Curriculum Integration

There are several ways to integrate this table into your curriculum.

1. **Ecology Studies:** The subject of this table offers a shorthand curriculum for environmental studies. Preparation of the exhibit, together with other activities in this chapter, gives children a good hands-on understanding of basic environmental issues.

2. **Earth Sciences:** This table offers an opportunity for discussion of the water cycle (toxic runoff and smog can affect the water in the water cycle by redistributing toxins far from their source), water delivery systems (aqueducts, wells), and conservation.

3. **Life Sciences:** Environmental studies logically lend themselves to discussions of dwindling habitats and attendant species endangerment. This can also lead to discussions of the adaptive abilities of animals as they learn to cope with urban development.

From *Classroom Museums: Touchable Tables for Kids*, published by GoodYear Books. Copyright © 1992 Pamela Marx.

# Table Appearance

*The table can be organized in three parts—recycling (waste/landfills), air quality, and water quality. The table text should be cut apart and displayed on the viewing side of the exhibit for ease of reading. Cover any wall facing the exhibit with environmental posters purchased or made by students.*

1. **Recycling:** Arrange examples of recyclables on the table—glass, aluminum, tin, paper, and plastic. Next, a comparative display of environmentally sound versus wasteful packaging is enlightening—for instance, chili in a can versus chili packaged for the microwave or a six-pack of plastic applesauce containers versus applesauce in a jar with a reusable plastic container and an airtight lid. Use the biodegradability study described in the table text. Put the survey results on a roll of paper at the back of the table. Tag notable items such as peeled versus whole fruit, plastic bagged versus loose materials. Tags should challenge students to think: Why is one piece of fruit more decayed than the other? Does burial in a plastic bag slow the decaying process? Which things should not go to a landfill?

2. **Air Quality:** The primary touchables here are the petroleum jelly air surveys described in the table text. A small branch of a tree or bush that grows near a well-traveled road or freeway is another good touchable. If you haven't had any rain for a while, the leaves get very dusty. You can also make smudge test strips. Have children look at home and at school for high ledges that are not cleaned frequently. With adult supervision (so that they don't touch an unpainted, splintery surface), children run white cotton balls over the ledge to test the dirtiness of the dust that collects there. The balls can be mounted on a paper or tagboard and identified as to the location from which each smudge is taken.

3. **Water Quality:** Gutter survey results as described in the table text make a good display on this part of the table. Place the material gathered on a roll of paper at the back of the table. Place tags on some of the items to suggest how they can hurt fish and animals with which they come in contact. For instance, six-pack plastic tops hook onto birds' beaks and animals' mouths and necks. Yogurt containers can trap the snouts of small animals as they forage for food. Inks in paper and residues in empty containers contaminate water and hurt fish.

From *Classroom Museums: Touchable Tables for Kids*, published by GoodYear Books. Copyright © 1992 Pamela Marx.

Use the mylar balloon experiment here, too. Fill a juice bottle with salt water and a piece of mylar. Let it sit for two weeks, shaking it occasionally. The mylar will begin to look like a jellyfish. Sea turtles can mistake mylar like this for food and become ill or die by eating it.

Use a comparative plant exhibit on this part of the table. Get examples of plants that require heavy watering and plants that are drought resistant. These plants, along with any water-saving paraphernalia like low-flow showerheads and toilet tank water bags make thought-provoking touchables related to water conservation.

## Sample Touchables

See discussions of sample touchables in the preceding section on Table Appearance and in individual sections of the table text.

## Student Involvement in Table Preparation

Students in all grades can participate in the creation of this exhibit. Most class curricula these days include the areas of conservation and ecology. As your class studies these areas and undertakes surveys and experiments, the results can become part of the exhibit. The table text for this chapter gives specific ideas for activities students can undertake to create nearly all the touchables. Additional student activities for use on the table are suggested in the Table Appearance section of this chapter.

From *Classroom Museums: Touchable Tables for Kids*, published by GoodYear Books. Copyright © 1992 Pamela Marx.

## Table Text

*While this table text offers specific touchable ideas, feel free to delete these and substitute other environmental experiments you prefer. Much of the informational value of this table exhibit can be conveyed through tags which bear thought-provoking environmental facts and questions.*

## Recycling

### Keeping Our Earth, Our Air, Our Water Healthy

We use many different things every day. We buy most of them. Most of these come in boxes and wrappings that we throw away.

Think of some of the things you used before you came to school today.

Did you eat breakfast? Did you eat cereal? What did the cereal come in when you bought it? Will you throw that away?

Did you eat a banana? Did you eat it all or did you throw part of it away? Or maybe you ate an apple or an orange?

Did you brush your teeth? What happened to the toothpaste you used? Where did it go? What was the toothpaste packaged in when you bought it?

Did you walk to school or did you ride in a car?

On this Earth, we live in what is called a closed environment. Living in a closed environment means that as we live on this earth we can use only the resources we have here. We can't go to Mars or Venus to get new resources if we run out of what we need. We are using some of our resources up quickly. We are polluting others. And still others we are wasting.

What are resources?

Resources are the things that we take from the earth and use. Water is a resource that we drink, bathe in and grow food with. Trees are a resource with which we build homes, make paper, and kindle fires in our fireplaces. Oil is a resource with which we run our cars, heat our homes, and make plastics and other synthetic and human-made products. How can we take care of all these resources that make up our Earth?

From *Classroom Museums: Touchable Tables for Kids*, published by GoodYear Books. Copyright © 1992 Pamela Marx.

From *Classroom Museums: Touchable Tables for Kids,* published by GoodYear Books. Copyright © 1992 Pamela Marx.

## Trash, Trash, and More Trash

*In the last half century, we have begun to enjoy the convenience of throw-away living. We buy a hamburger and throw away the wrapper. The toaster or hair dryer breaks and we throw it away. We use disposable razors, disposable cameras, and disposable diapers. We buy products that are packaged in many layers—a cardboard box fitted with an interior bag and covered by plastic. Do we have to throw away all this trash? Is there anything else we can do with it? Why should we bother? Think about these things:*

- *American people and businesses generate 160 million tons of garbage each year. Garbage is called solid waste. Where does it all go?*

- *Americans throw away 24 million tons of yard waste such as lawn clippings and leaves each year. What can we do with these wastes?*

- *We save one 50-gallon barrel of oil for every 125 pounds of paper that we recycle. The average American uses this much paper each year. Why throw it away when so much of it can be recycled?*

## What is a landfill?

When we throw something away, where does it go? Most of what we throw away goes to the dump. Dump is another word for landfill. What is a landfill? It is really just a very, very big hole in the ground. The big hole is usually a natural depression in the landscape that is surrounded by hills. It holds our trash. All around the country, landfills are getting full. We have more and more trouble finding space for new ones.

How can we keep dumps from filling up so fast? We can do several things. We can:

- Recycle
- Reduce and Reuse—Change our buying and lifestyle habits.

## What is recycling?

Recycling is many things. We most often think of recycling as taking used or empty aluminum, glass, and tin containers and newspaper to someone who will make new products out of them. How does this work?

Recycling **aluminum** is the process of melting it down and pressing the molten or melted metal into sheets that can be made into new cans.

Recycling **glass** is the process of crushing it into small pieces and melting them down to make new glass.

Recycling **paper** is the process of turning it into pulp and making new paper from that pulp.

## Why is recycling a good thing to do?

It saves space and it saves our resources. When we recycle newspaper, we save trees from being cut down to make wood pulp. When we recycle aluminum or glass, we not only save new resources in the earth from being used, we save energy because making new cans or bottles from old ones does not use as much energy as making new containers from raw materials. When we use fewer manufacturing processes, we create less air and water pollution. Think about these things:

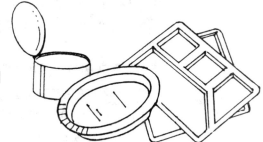

- Using recycled aluminum cuts down air pollution from aluminum products by 65 percent. Making products from recycled aluminum uses only about 5 percent (1/20th) of the energy required to mine and manufacture raw materials to make new aluminum products.

- Recycling one glass jar can save enough energy to light a 100-watt light bulb for four hours.

- Making new paper from recycled paper uses one third less energy than making paper from new wood pulp. Recycling paper also cuts air pollution by 95 percent and water pollution by 35 percent.

Do these seem like good reasons to recycle?

## What does it mean to change your buying and lifestyle habits?

When we change our buying and lifestyle habits, we reduce the amount of things we use and the trash we make. We also find ways to reuse things we have. How does this work?

Take a look at what you buy. Take a look at your trash. Think about some of these things:

1. Are some of the foods you buy packaged in several different layers? So much of our trash is packaging—that is, the papers, foils, and plastics in which our food is wrapped. Think about rice, for example. Microwavable rice might come packaged in two or three layers. Quick rice might be packaged in one box. Can you reduce the trash you create by watching out for product packaging?

2. Do you ever throw old clothes or shoes away? Can they be reused by someone else? Maybe you can pass them down to a cousin or donate them to a needy family. This is really just another kind of recycling. It is the kind that requires you to change your habits a little bit.

3. If you have a wood or metal object in your yard, how can you make it last longer so you don't have to buy a new one? If you replace things less often, you save resources, energy, and landfill space, too. If you paint it, will it last longer? Sometimes just taking good care of the things we have can help the environment by reducing the amount of trash we make.

4. If you have an appliance that isn't working, can you repair it? If you can't, should you throw it away or try to donate it to a charity that will repair and reuse it?

5. Do you ever buy something in a plastic squeeze bottle rather than a glass bottle? Which one is easier for you to recycle? When you buy something, look at its container. If you have a choice between a container you can recycle and one that you must throw away, buy the recyclable one.

6. Do you have to throw away lawn clippings, or can you do something else with them? What makes lawn clippings different from some of your other trash? Lawn clippings are biodegradable. That means they break down naturally in the environment. Rather than sending your lawn clippings to the dump, compost them in your yard. They will decay and become nutrients to enrich your soil.

From *Classroom Museums: Touchable Tables for Kids*, published by GoodYear Books. Copyright © 1992 Pamela Marx.

When you examine your habits to see how you can change them to help the environment, it helps to know which things are biodegradable and which things are not.

Let's look at the things on this table. What things are biodegradable? How long will it take them to decompose? Does it take some things longer than others?

Think about:

1. Plastic containers, wrap, bottles, bags, markers
2. Glass jars, containers, bottles
3. Aluminum cans, foil, pie plates, copper pennies, other coins, paper clips
4. Paper cups, newspaper, recycled paper, computer paper
5. Leaves, grass clippings, dead branches
6. Table scraps, fruit peels, whole fruit.

The things on this table represent a *trash biodegradability survey*. Small pieces of many different items were buried for a period of at least one month. Which things are starting to decompose? Do any of the results surprise you? If trash is enclosed in a plastic bag, does this affect the decaying process? Does whole fruit decay at the same rate as parts of fruit?

## Other Environmental Issues

*We worry a lot about trash. We hear a lot about recycling. What other problems do we have with our environment?*

### Is Our Air Clean?

Many things go into our air each day. The cars we drive emit exhaust into the air. Factories, manufacturing plants, and oil refineries spew smoke into the air. Some of the aerosol cleaning and household sprays we use release chemicals into the air. Large and small things that we use and rely on each day put pollutants into the air. These pollutants are not healthy. Some of them, like dust and fiber, are visible. Others, like hydrocarbons and ozone, are not. In order to keep the air safe for all living things, we adopt laws to limit the pollutants that go into the air. But still, the air in some cities is dirty.

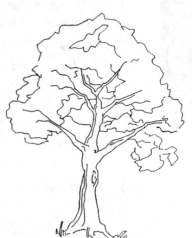

How clean or dirty is the air where you live? Is it different depending upon where you live in your community? Look at the exhibits on this table. The insides of several empty white plastic margarine or frozen topping containers were smeared with petroleum jelly. These containers were then placed outside in trees or bushes or on top of fences for one month. When the containers were collected again, we were able to see where the air in our community is cleanest and where it seems dirtiest.

Does it seem cleaner near a park? Does it seem dirtier near a freeway or other heavily travelled road? Does it seem cleaner near a school? Does it seem dirtier near a factory? What do the air samples tell you about the air in your community?

From *Classroom Museums: Touchable Tables for Kids,* published by GoodYear Books. Copyright © 1992 Pamela Marx.

What can we do to help keep the air as clean as possible?

1. We can plant trees. Trees process the air in the atmosphere around them and make new oxygen. Trees help keep the air clean and healthy.

2. We can walk whenever possible. If we can think of ways to use our cars less, we will help keep the air clean. Can you walk somewhere instead of driving? If you are driving, can you combine several errands on one trip so you don't drive as much? Doing these things also helps save gasoline which is another resource we take from the earth.

3. We can be careful about the products we buy. Use products with fewer chemicals. If we use more natural products, fewer chemicals are released into the air when the products are made, and fewer chemicals are released into the air as we use the products.

## Is Our Water Clean?

Water, like air, is necessary for all living things on earth to survive. Salt water is found in oceans. Ocean water serves as a habitat for marine life. Fresh water is found in lakes and rivers, in glaciers and underground (groundwater). Fresh water is the kind of water we drink. All of this water, ocean or fresh, needs to be clean. It needs to be clean for people to drink and clean for fish and marine animals to live healthy lives.

## How does the water on our Earth get dirty?

Sometimes it gets dirty the same way air does. Manufacturing, industrial, and transporting operations located near or traveling across ocean or lake waters discharge unsafe fluids into the water. We have laws to limit these practices, but sometimes people make mistakes. Accidents happen, or equipment breaks and spills result.

Water gets dirty in other ways, too. Sometimes chemicals in a landfill soak into the soil and contaminate underground water. Sometimes litter and other wastes discarded by careless people make ocean, lake, and river waters dirty.

Since we can do something about litter every day, let's think about how litter affects water on our earth. Our litter can be carried into the ocean or a lake even if we live a great distance from the shore. Litter that goes down a storm drain often ends up in the ocean or a lake. It travels there through a complicated network of underground pipes. What kind of litter collects on the street in front of your local storm drains? Would these things be good for fish and other animals that live in oceans and lakes? Take a survey of litter that finds its way into a gutter. Collect litter from one strip of gutter for one week. This litter could eventually end up in the ocean.

What kinds of litter do you see in your gutter survey? There might be papers, foam cups, plastic six-pack tops, broken balloons. All of this litter was collected from one gutter. None of it is good for animals. Six-pack tops get caught on birds' beaks and animals' snouts. Broken balloons look like food to fish. If a fish eats the balloon, it becomes very ill or dies.

What else can affect our water? Sometimes people and businesses put things into street gutters that can be even more harmful than litter. Have you ever seen someone change the oil in a car and wash the dirty oil away in the gutter? This used oil is a toxic substance that is harmful. When that oil leaves the gutter, is it really gone? Where does it go?

Sometimes people throw away pesticides and solvents incorrectly. Instead of sending these things to special places, they send them to regular dumps. Chemicals and poisons can seep into the soil under a dump to contaminate underground water. Then the water is not safe to drink.

From *Classroom Museums: Touchable Tables for Kids*, published by GoodYear Books. Copyright © 1992 Pamela Marx.

## What can we do to help keep water clean?

1. We can always pick up litter when we see it. This will keep it from being washed to the ocean in our storm drains.

2. When we have a balloon, we can keep hold of it. Sometimes helium balloons are lost in the air. These can end up in ocean waters and be eaten by unsuspecting animals.

3. We can make sure we dispose of liquid wastes the right way. If we change oil in our cars, we should never put it in the gutter. We should never wash old paint down the gutter. If we clean with chemical cleaners, we should never throw the dirty residues out in the gutter.

4. Throw away paints, solvents, and pesticides by sending them to the right place. These kinds of things should not be thrown away with our regular trash. Because they can be toxic to animals and can seep into the soil if they go to regular landfills, there are special places to dispose of these kinds of wastes.

5. Recycle! 3.3 billion pounds of toxic chemicals are released into water each year in paper bleaching processes. Products from recycled paper require little or no bleaching. Recycling paper cuts water pollution by as much as 35 percent.

## Are there any other ways in which our water needs help?

Yes. We need to conserve our water. What does it mean to conserve? Conservation means saving water. It means saving it whenever we can. In some parts of the country, water conservation is very important because of conditions like drought. What can we do to help conserve water?

• We can take shorter showers and use less water in baths.

• We can fix faucets so they do not leak. One leaky faucet can waste twenty to fifty gallons of water a day.

• We can plant drought-resistant plants so we needn't water them as much.

• We can use special shower heads and faucets that reduce the amount of water that comes out of the faucet.

• We can turn off the water while we brush our teeth.

• We can install water bags in our toilets so that each flush uses less water.

## What Can We Do Every Day to Help Have a Clean Environment?

**Think** about the things we buy, the things we throw away, the things we do.

**Watch** what others do and remind them to throw away litter, safely dispose of wastes, and buy safe products.

**Act** carefully in everything we do, always remembering our important part in keeping the world clean.

From *Classroom Museums: Touchable Tables for Kids*, published by GoodYear Books. Copyright © 1992 Pamela Marx.

## Teacher Resources

---

### Discussion Guidelines

*Use these discussion guidelines to stimulate student thinking about environmentally sound practices at home and school. These guidelines lend themselves especially well to teacher use.*

What is waste?

> *Trash, garbage, solid waste*
> *Sewage—liquid and semisolid wastes*

What kinds of trash do you throw away at home? At school?
Where do these things go?

> *To the dump.*

What is a landfill? Is it a dump?

> *Landfill is another word for dump. It is a large depression in the ground that is surrounded by higher ground.*

What happens when a landfill fills up?
Then where does trash go?

> *We have to find new landfills.*

Do we have room for more landfills?

> *No. Space is getting harder to find.*

If we don't have room for more landfills, what can we do to keep them from filling up so fast?

- *Reduce*
  *Buy products with less packaging.*
  *Take care of things so they last longer.*
- *Reuse*
  *Hand down clothes so that they are used again.*
  *Try to save wrapping paper on gifts you get.*
  *Use it again on other gifts.*
  *Use both sides of paper, not just one.*
- *Recycle*

Can we recycle?

What is recycling?

> *Saving something and using it again for another purpose.*

What are some of the things you can recycle?

> *Newspaper    Glass         Aluminum*
> *Tin              Plastic bags*
> *Some plastic containers*

What can you do about things you can't recycle? How can we cut down on waste from these things?

What about used clothing? What can be done with it?

> *Reuse it.        Donate it.        Hand it down.*

Can you change your buying habits?

> *Reduce.*
> *Watch the layers of packaging on the things you buy.*
> *Buy things made of recycled products.*

What if you have a choice between buying something in a recyclable or non-recyclable container? Which would you buy?

Much of our trash is packaging. How many layers of packaging are there in the things you buy?

> [Note: *Show examples. For instance, many microwave items have several layers of packaging and a disposable container.*]

Why is recycling a good thing to do?

> *Fewer things go to landfills.*
> *Things are used again and not wasted.*

What do we save by recycling?

> *Landfill space   Energy         Resources*

What other things do we need to worry about in our environment?

> *Air              Water          Habitats*

What about our air?

How does it get dirty or smoggy?

> *Factory emissions*
> *Car exhaust*
> *Household cleaner and solvent emissions*

How can we help the air?

> *Walk more; drive less.*
> *Buy household products carefully; look for natural products.*

What about our water?

We have several water worries.

> *Polluted oceans*
> *Polluted lakes and rivers*
> *Polluted underground water*

From *Classroom Museums: Touchable Tables for Kids,* published by GoodYear Books. Copyright © 1992 Pamela Marx.

Why is water pollution a problem?

*Kills animal life*

*Makes drinking water unsafe*

*Makes fish and other seafoods unsafe to eat*

What causes the pollution?

*Litter*

*Factory wastes*

*Careless people who dispose of harmful liquids improperly*

*Chemicals in landfills that soak into the soil and taint underground water*

How can you help?

*Pick up litter.*

*Be careful about your buying habits.*

*Remind adults not to dispose of wastes improperly.*

*Recycle.*

*Do not dispose of harmful chemicals in your trash.*

What else can we do for our water?

*Conserve*

*Water less*

*Toilet bags*

*Low-flow fixtures*

*Fix leaks*

## Student Activities

1. Have an environmental poster contest. Encourage each child to think of a clean-up slogan relating to things everyone can do to create a cleaner environment. Display posters around the school for an Earth Week or Earth Day celebration.

2. Ask the children, either as a class or individually, to create environmental alphabets. Begin with phrases like "A is for acid rain, which hurts plants and animals," or "B is for Be careful to always throw litter away." Perhaps you can use your environmental alphabet as a jumping off point for an environmental newsletter for school Earth Day celebrations.

   A newsletter can include: student reports on current recycling efforts on campus; surveys of classroom trash generation; interviews with school or city officials on ways the school or students can help the environment; environmental facts researched by the students; and "person-in-the-street" question surveys of students. (What do you do at home for the environment? If you could give the earth an environmental gift, what would it be?)

3. Write an environmental pledge or letter of concern to a local city official. This project helps bring the governmental process alive for children. Local politicians are likely to respond more quickly than political officials working far away.

## Resources

1. Local utilities often have free posters and charts of the water cycle, local water delivery and treatment system, and conservation ideas. Check with them for posters, water- and energy-saving touchables, and possible exhibit speakers versed in conservation and pollution issues.

2. Local city offices usually have environmental or recycling units that are happy to make presentations on environmental issues. Sometimes they have pamphlets and flyers available for the children to take home.

3. Some large national businesses are developing task forces to speak to organizations and schools about their environmental efforts. McDonald's Corporation has commenced such a program in some parts of the country. Ask your local franchise if such a program is available in your community.

4. Good resource books for student environmental projects are:

   *Earth Book for Kids* by Linda Schwartz, published by The Learning Works (1990) (highly recommended).

   *Environmental Science: 49 Science Fair Projects* by Robert L. Bonnet and G. Daniel Keen, published by Tab Books (1990).

   *Save the Earth: An Action Handbook for Kids* by Betty Miles, published by Alfred A. Knopf (1991).

   *50 Simple Things Kids Can Do to Save the Earth* by The Earthworks Group, published by Andrews & McMeel (1990).

From *Classroom Museums: Touchable Tables for Kids*, published by GoodYear Books. Copyright © 1992 Pamela Marx.

**Recycling Puzzle**

## Color the recycling arrows.

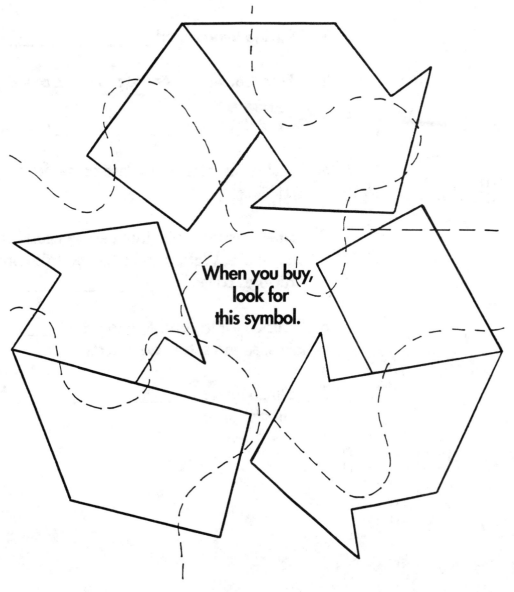

When you buy,
look for
this symbol.

**Glue the puzzle to construction paper. Cut out on dotted puzzle lines.**

From *Classroom Museums: Touchable Tables for Kids*, published by GoodYear Books. Copyright © 1992 Pamela Marx.

**Water**

*Name*_____ *Date*_____

_____

## Water—We need water and we need it clean
Can you fill in the blanks in these water facts?
- Water • Rivers • Aqueducts • Pollute • Groundwater
- Wells • Unhealthy

1. All living things need _____ to survive.

2. Water that lies under the ground is called _____.

3. People dig _____ in order to use groundwater.

4. Some water that people use comes from _____ and lakes.

5. Sometimes the water that people need is not located where the people are. Water can be moved from one place to another by structures called _____.

6. Pesticides, litter, and sewage can _____water in lakes, streams, and aqueducts.

7. Polluted water is _____ for people, plants, and animals.

# Answer Key

## Marine Life

1. Fish
2. Starfish
3. Anemone
4. Crab
5. Octopus
6. Clam
7. Shark

    Invertebrates: starfish, octopus, clam, crab, and anemone.

## Mollusks

Univalve mollusks shown:

Cone, margarite, triton, abalone

Mollusks that have no shells: octopus, squid

## Reptiles

1. Snake
2. Lizard

## Mammals All, But Who Are We?

### Tracks

1. Deer
2. Raccoon
3. Beaver
4. Field Mouse
5. Skunk
6. Wolf

### Description

1. Beaver
2. Deer
3. Field Mouse
4. Raccoon
5. Wolf
6. Skunk

From *Classroom Museums: Touchable Tables for Kids*, published by GoodYear Books. Copyright © 1992 Pamela Marx.

## Colors I

Primary colors: Red, Yellow, Blue

Secondary colors: Orange, Green, Purple

You make a secondary color by mixing two primary colors.

## Colors II

A blend of two primary colors complements the third.

## Holiday Matching

1. India
2. African-American
3. Japan
4. Mexico
5. Scotland
6. Sweden
7. China
8. Holland
9. Vietnam

1. Mexico
2. France
3. United States
4. Italy
5. Holland
6. Germany

   Diwali, Oshogatsu, Hogmanay, Sun Nin and Tet celebrate the new year.

## Using Prey

Possible answers:

1. Hide
2. Bones, Teeth
3. Meat
4. Hooves
5. Hide
6. Antlers
7. Antlers
8. Hide
9. Bones, Teeth

From *Classroom Museums: Touchable Tables for Kids*, published by GoodYear Books. Copyright © 1992 Pamela Marx.

## From Cacao Bean to Chocolate Bar

1. Cacao beans are harvested from cacao pods.
2. Cacao beans are fermented, roasted, and winnowed.
3. Cacao beans are ground.
4. Chocolate liquor is mixed with sugar, cocoa butter, and flavorings.
5. Chocolate is molded into desired shape.

## The Early Travels of Chocolate

1. Mexico
2. Spain
3. Europe
4. American

## Water

1. Water
2. Groundwater
3. Wells
4. Rivers
5. Aqueducts
6. Pollute
7. Unhealthy

From *Classroom Museums: Touchable Tables for Kids*, published by GoodYear Books. Copyright © 1992 Pamela Marx.

FRANKLIN PIERCE COLLEGE LIBRARY

00103778

DATE DUE

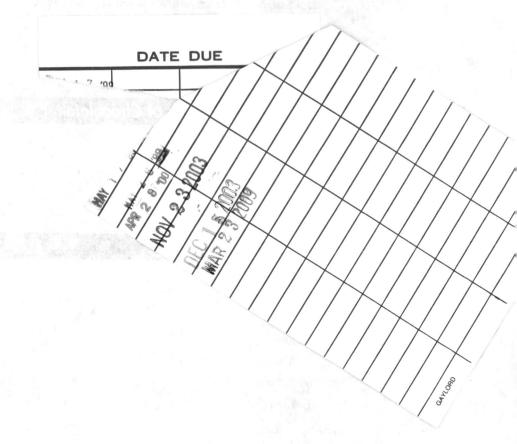

MAY 1 7 '00

MAY 1 8 '00
APR 2 8 '00
NOV 2 3 2003
DEC 1 5 2003
MAR 2 3 2009

GAYLORD